PRAYER AND THE END OF DAYS

PRAYING GOD'S PURPOSES IN TROUBLED TIMES

DAVID BUTTS

PRAYERSHOP
PUBLISHING

Terre Haute, Indiana

PrayerShop Publishing is the publishing arm of Harvest Prayer Ministries and the Church Prayer Leaders Network. Harvest Prayer Ministries exists to transform lives through teaching prayer. Its online prayer store, www.prayer-shop.org, has more than 600 prayer resources available for purchase.

ISBN: 9781935012085

Library of Congress Control Number: 2009904212

1 2 3 4 5 6 7 | 2015 2014 2013 2012 2011 2010 2009

CONTENTS

FOREWORD

I grew up in a denomination that had as one of its primary emphases, the second coming of Christ. Jesus was our coming king. Everything we did in evangelism and missions was undergirded by the catchphrase: "Bring Back the King."

This was due to the truth of Matthew 24:14: "And this gospel of the kingdom will be preached in the whole world as a testimony to all nations, and then the end will come." The Bible teaches that there would be an "end of days"—at least on the earth as we know it. And evangelization would play a part in it.

Our church people were interested in biblical prophecy and speakers on this subject were popular. We watched Israel and world events with interest. We were conscious of wars and rumors of wars, of increases in earthquakes, floods, and natural disasters. But there was a stronger interest in missions and world evangelization. How many more people groups needed to be reached. When would that last tribe hear the gospel? That would be the ultimate sign of Jesus' soon appearance.

You see, we did not want to fight against the second coming of Christ. We wanted to speed it up. Everything we did was to move the kingdom forward.

Today, we are living in troubled times. Financial crisis that is nearing Depression Era situation. A madman in Iran possibly with nuclear power. Hatred toward believers is growing at an alarming rate in the United States. The moral compass of our nation is seemingly beyond repair.

Many believers are despairing. Many do not know what to do. There is a growing sense of gloom. But that is not the posture we should take. If indeed the second coming of Christ is imminent, should we not long for it, embrace it, work toward it, pray for it?

If that is the correct posture to take, then we should look with great interest—not despair—at world events. What is God orchestrating? How can I be a kingdom-minded believer and pray and work toward God's purposes?

That's why I love this book. Dave Butts has taken that approach. We should not fear the end but should increase our prayer efforts, our evangelism efforts, our kingdom efforts.

Prayer and the End of Days offers practical everyday suggestions on how we as believers can pray the purposes of God in troubled times. Rather than lose faith and be discouraged, the activity this book encourages will increase faith and develop believers who ill once again keep "their eyes on the skies."

Every true believer needs to read *Prayer and the End of Days*. Then they need to put into practice its prayer suggestions. The church and the world—and you—will be better off for it.

Jonathan Graf
Church Prayer Leaders Network
Founder, *Pray!* magazine

INTRODUCTION

I am very grateful that I was raised in a Christian home by godly parents who brought me up in the faith. One of the things for which I'm especially thankful is a father who believed in the Lord's soon return and trained me to be watchful. I remember many times Dad would call me into the living room to see something on the television news. "David," he would say, "this event just might be a fulfillment of a certain prophecy." And then he would open Scripture and show me a prophecy that spoke of events that must take place before Jesus' return. What a wonderful way to grow up in the faith!

I'm convinced that one of the great needs of the church today is just such a belief in the imminent return of the Lord. Apart from that, we focus far too much on the problems and obstacles in our faith and lose sight of the glorious goal of our life in Christ. It is too easy to forget the eternal aspect of the Christian faith and the victorious end of human history as seen in Scripture.

The early church serves as a good model of those who had a balanced concept of the Lord's return. They kept their eyes on the skies, awaiting the anytime return of Jesus, while at the same time focusing on the needs of those around them. They were excited about heaven, but did not fail to carry out the work of the kingdom of God on earth. Their eager anticipation of the Lord's return provided them with a powerful motivation for holiness and effective service. It should motivate us as well.

Jesus told the apostles, "If I go and prepare a place for you, I will come back and take you to be with me that you also may be where I am" (John 14:3). At Jesus' ascension into heaven, the angels said to the disciples, "Men of Galilee . . . why do you stand here looking into the sky? This same Jesus, who has been taken from you into heaven, will come back in the same way you have seen him go into heaven" (Acts 1:11).

From that point on, the church has awaited the Lord's return with great anticipation. Far from a side issue, the second coming of Christ was a central theme in the teaching of the apostles. In Peter's sermon on the day of Pentecost, he spoke of the events of that day as that which must occur "before the coming of the great and glorious day of the Lord" (Acts 2:20).

Peter continued that emphasis in his letters. In his first letter he wrote, "The end of all things is near. Therefore be clear minded and self-controlled so that you can pray" (4:7). Peter's second letter again stresses our quality of life in anticipation of the Lord's return: ". . . since you are looking forward to this [the Second Coming], make every effort to be found spotless, blameless and at peace with him" (3:14). I believe it is vitally important for the church today to see the total lack of speculation concerning times and seasons in Peter's writings. His focus is on a lifestyle impacted by the anticipation of Jesus' return.

The apostle Paul has the same emphasis in his writings. He gives instructions to Timothy regarding his preaching "in view of his [Jesus'] appearing and his kingdom" (2 Timothy 4:1). Paul writes to the Thessalonian church, which is overly concerned with speculation regarding the timing of the Second Coming. In 1 Thessalonians 4:13–5:11, he devotes a whole section to teaching on the Lord's return with the practical admonition to "be alert and self-controlled" (5:6) and to "encourage one another" (5:11) regarding His return.

Paul begins his second letter to the Thessalonians with the powerful word picture, "when the Lord Jesus is revealed from heaven in blazing fire with his powerful angels" (1:7). He continues on throughout the second chapter, teaching about the Second Coming and encouraging the believers to stand firm in their doctrine concerning Jesus' return.

One passage that gives us great insight into the importance of belief in the imminent return of the Lord to the early church is found in Paul's letter to Titus. Paul writes of the grace of God that calls us to "live self-controlled, upright and godly lives in this present age, while we wait for the blessed hope—the glorious appearing of our great God and Savior, Jesus Christ" (2:12–13). Again the focus is on the lifestyle of the waiting Christian.

The phrase "wait for the blessed hope" is important. Too many Christians today seem to dread the Lord's return. At the very least it is viewed as relatively unimportant in light of the critical issues we face today. We are to be a people so completely and utterly in love with Jesus that the desire of our lives is to see Him face-to-face. It is this kind of passion that allows Paul to write of His appearing as our "blessed hope."

Eager anticipation of His return helps us live lives of holiness and purity. As the bride of Christ looks forward to her reunion with the Bridegroom, she will greatly desire to be found dressed in white, without spot or blemish. Anticipation also can serve as a wonderful motivator for personal evangelism and acts of prayer and service that extend the kingdom of God.

Peter helps us close out our thinking on this in the third chapter of his second letter. He points out that the delay in the Lord's return is only because His love is so great that He is "not wanting anyone to perish, but everyone to come to repentance" (2 Peter 3:9). Both God's role and ours are stressed as he continues on: "Since everything will be destroyed in this way, what kind of people ought you to be? You ought to live holy and godly lives as you look forward to the day of God and speed its coming. That day will bring about the destruction of the heavens by fire, and the elements will melt in the heat. But in keeping with his promise we are looking forward to a new heaven and a new earth, the home of righteousness" (2 Peter 3:11–13). May we join our prayers with the saints of all ages who have prayed, "Come, Lord Jesus" (Revelation 22:20).

This book is not intended to be predictive in nature. However, I personally believe that we are living in a period of time toward the end of the last days. I recognize that many who have gone before me have also thought that and been wrong. I'm okay with being wrong; however, I plan on living as though the Lord may return at any time. The purpose of this book is to help train the followers of Jesus to pray in an informed way as they see events unfold that may lead to the Lord's return.

Whether or not Jesus returns within my lifetime, the issues that are dealt with in the following chapters are being faced currently by Christians today. As the Day of the Lord approaches, these issues and crises will increase. With that, the need for powerful prayer and holy living will also increase. Because this need for prayer will continue to grow and evolve as situations change on the world scene, I invite you to stay in touch as we grow together. Check out our website: www.prayerandendofdays.com. It's a place for discussion and further communication for those who are praying in preparation for the Lord's return.

Chapter One

LOOKING FORWARD TO HIS RETURN

I love to talk and write about the return of Jesus to this planet. Talk (not argue), mind you, although there are many Christians who think arguing is what we are to do. From childhood I was taught to look forward to the return of Jesus. There are many passages of Scripture that speak of His Second Coming. Here's my favorite:

> First of all, you must understand that in the last days scoffers will come, scoffing and following their own evil desires. They will say, "Where is this 'coming' he promised? Ever since our fathers died, everything goes on as it has since the beginning of creation." But they deliberately forget that long ago by God's word the heavens existed and the earth was formed out of water and by water. By these waters also the world of that time was deluged and destroyed. By the same word the present heavens and earth are reserved for fire, being kept for the day of judgment and destruction of ungodly men.
>
> But do not forget this one thing, dear friends: With the Lord a day is like a thousand years, and a thousand

years are like a day. The Lord is not slow in keeping his promise, as some understand slowness. He is patient with you, not wanting anyone to perish, but everyone to come to repentance.

But the day of the Lord will come like a thief. The heavens will disappear with a roar; the elements will be destroyed by fire, and the earth and everything in it will be laid bare.

Since everything will be destroyed in this way, what kind of people ought you to be? You ought to live holy and godly lives as you look forward to the day of God and speed its coming. That day will bring about the destruction of the heavens by fire, and the elements will melt in the heat. But in keeping with his promise we are looking forward to a new heaven and a new earth, the home of righteousness.

So then, dear friends, since you are looking forward to this, make every effort to be found spotless, blameless and at peace with him. (2 Peter 3:3–14)

The passage says, "as you look forward to the day of God." Are you looking forward to the return of Jesus? I think a lot of Christians are afraid to say no to that question. They instinctively know that the answer should be "yes, of course I'm looking forward to His return." But in our heart of hearts is that really so? Are we longing for His return?

If we are not looking forward to the Lord's return, we will not be serious about prayer that prepares us for that great event. We will never make the effort to give ourselves to the awesome issues of intercession that can usher in His appearance again on planet Earth if we are not looking forward to it. This book will be nothing more than an academic exercise unless we have somehow moved into a place of eager expectation.

All too often it seems that we have made our home here on this planet, and heaven is sort of a safety net to catch us when we die. Occasionally, the death of a loved one wrenches our sight off the affairs of this world long enough to remind us that there is a heaven. Most of the time, however, we find ourselves firmly ensconced in the daily matters of this life.

Some would ask, "What's the problem with that? Do you want us to be so heavenly minded that we are of no earthly good?" My problem is that the New Testament church seemed to be far more focused on the return of Jesus than is the church today. And that focus served the early church well. It gave believers a passion and urgency so that within a generation it was said of them, "They have turned the world upside down."

The emphasis on the Lord's return is not for the purpose of speculation concerning dates or developing systems of what His return will be like. Those matters can be interesting but can become distractions if we are not careful. Divisions that grieve the Lord can arise over various viewpoints.

The apostle Peter instead gives us a clear, balanced picture of how a proper emphasis on the return of Jesus can impact the church. It is first of all a matter of looking forward to His return. If repetition is a way of making a point, Peter hammers home the matter of looking forward to the Second Coming:

1. "As you look forward" (2 Peter 3:12)

2. "We are looking forward" (2 Peter 3:13)
3. "Since you are looking forward to this" (2 Peter 3:14)

This emphasis on looking forward to the return of Jesus is to have a practical impact on the character and lifestyle of the Christian. Peter asks, "what kind of people ought you to be?" And then he answers, "You ought to live holy and godly lives as you look forward to the day of God" (2 Peter 3:11–12). In verse 14 he phrases it differently, but with the same result: "since you are looking forward to this, make every effort to be found spotless, blameless and at peace with him." Could it be that we do not look forward to Christ's coming because we do not want to change our lifestyles? There is one other lifestyle change that is encouraged by looking forward to the Second Coming. As we begin to realize that this world is temporary, we find ourselves more urgently involved in completing the task of world evangelization. Whether it is in sharing our faith with a neighbor or in giving financially to fund a missionary, we will throw ourselves wholeheartedly into this as a result of a life of expectancy.

Throughout this passage, we see the Lord's concern for the lost. In 2 Peter 3:9, Peter points out that He does not want anyone to perish, but desires them to come to repentance. Verse 12 includes the fascinating admonition that we may help speed the coming of the day of God. Most scholars believe that this means making sure we are involved in finishing the task of world evangelization. It fits well with Matthew 24:14: "And this gospel of the kingdom will be preached in the whole world as a testimony to all nations, and then the end will come."

William Carey said, "If you want the Kingdom speeded, go out and speed it yourselves. Only obedience rationalizes prayer.

Only Missions can redeem your intercessions from insincerity" (see "Quotes" at www.watchword.org). Andrew Murray stated, "There is need of a great revival of spiritual life, of truly fervent devotion to our Lord Jesus, of entire consecration to His service. It is only in a church in which this spirit of revival has at least begun, that there is any hope of radical change in the relation of the majority of our Christian people to mission work . . ." (see "Quotes" at www.watchword.org). Are you looking forward to the return of Jesus? Many Christians would automatically reply, "Of course!" But is that an honest answer, carefully thought through and borne out as true by our actions? Many times we answer how we think we ought to answer rather than how we actually feel.

Do you want Jesus to return soon? Are you praying according to scripture, "Come soon, Lord Jesus!"? Could it be instead that most of us would pray in our heart of hearts, "Not yet, Lord Jesus. Not yet!"?

Why would Christians, those called to be the bride of Christ, not desire passionately to be united forever with their Lord? I believe there are at least three reasons for this.

CONCERN FOR UNSAVED LOVED ONES

I put concern for unsaved loved ones first because I believe it to be the best of the possible reasons. All Christians have loved ones who do not know the Lord and greatly desire their salvation. For this reason, instead of longing for the Lord's return, many find themselves asking the Lord to delay His return.

The problem with this is twofold. First, the Christian is commanded to look forward to the Day of the Lord. It's hard to look forward to something when, in fact, you are dreading the possibility of being separated from loved ones for eternity. The second and perhaps most critical problem is that it demonstrates a lack of trust in the lordship of God's timing. Scripture already teaches us that God is not slow concerning the end, but is delaying because He wants people to come to repentance. We must take Him at His word, believing that He knows when the full measure of the harvest has come in and when it is time to bring down the curtain on this current age.

When we pray, "Come soon, Lord Jesus!" we are expressing our faith in His omnipotence and sovereignty. And until He comes, we have the opportunity and the responsibility to share our faith and lead others to Christ.

LOVE OF THIS WORLD

Christians often struggle with the imminence of heaven because they are too much at home in this world. That is especially true of those who have an abundance of possessions and privileges. If we are not careful, we can find ourselves grieving over the very thought of leaving all of this. Here is an indication of a clear lack of understanding of both the beauty and majesty of heaven, as well as a lack of love for the presence of the Lord.

One very subtle type of this error can be found in those not longing for heaven because of their love of ministry on earth. They rationalize, "But Lord, *I'm* not done yet. There is still so much left for *me* to do." When will we be done? Again, if we're not careful, we can find ourselves more in love with serving God than with loving God Himself.

The apostle Paul certainly loved serving the Lord, but he loved the Lord more than he loved his service to Him. Paul spoke of his desire to be with the Lord as "better by far" (Philippians 1:23). He was willing to remain on earth and serve if that was what the Lord wanted, but his true desire was simply to be with the Lord. This is the attitude that we must develop.

LACK OF PERSONAL HOLINESS

I believe, tragically, that the most common reason Christians do not desire the coming of the Lord is their lack of personal holiness. The passages from Second Peter at the beginning of this chapter stress that, in anticipation of the Lord's return, we are to live holy and godly lives. In addition, we are told to be spotless, blameless, and at peace with Him. Herein lies the problem. We are not ready for Jesus' return because our lives do not match up with the clear commands of Scripture.

We can have growing local churches and still not be ready for the Lord's return. We can have Bible studies and small groups and still not be ready for the Lord's return. We can have inspiring programs and conferences and still not be ready for the Lord's return. It is only as the very life of Jesus Himself begins to be demonstrated in us through holiness and godliness that we will find ourselves in eager anticipation of the Second Coming of Christ.

The life of holiness is not the perfect life. Many believers fall into a trap over this issue because they know the impossibility of attaining absolute perfection in this life. Therefore, they rationalize that there is no use in striving for holiness. Holiness, according to the best scriptural sense of the word, means to be set apart for a purpose. Christians are those who have been set apart to love, serve, and worship the Lord. Those who take this seriously will endeavor to put aside any sin that hinders them from a life lived fully for God.

When sin enters in (and it will), there should always be an

immediate grief over the sin leading to confession (agreement with God) and repentance. The life of holiness for the believer is as much about knowing what to do about sin in his or her life as it is in avoiding sin. True grief over sin, leading to confession and repentance, will train a Christian over a period of time to hate sin and attempt to avoid it at all costs.

Holiness is a process that is perfected only as we shed this fleshly body and stand before our Lord face-to-face. Longing for holiness and depending upon the Spirit of God to lead us away from sin and toward the Lord will create in us a great desire to see Him in the splendor of His holiness. We will be at peace with Him, our sins covered by the precious blood of Jesus, creating within us the ability to look forward to the day of God and speed its coming.

If you see yourself reflected in any of these three areas listed above, would you pray for a complete change of heart "while we wait for the blessed hope—the glorious appearing of our great God and Savior, Jesus Christ" (Titus 2:13)? Come soon, Lord Jesus!

As the longing to see Jesus face-to-face begins to grow in our lives, we will find ourselves beginning to pray, what might seem at first to be, unusual prayers. We will not simply pray more often, "Come soon, Lord Jesus." We will watch the news or read the newspaper and find ourselves deep in intercession. Issues surrounding Israel and the Middle East will begin to find their way into our prayer times. We will make connections with others who are standing on the wall of prayer for their nation and the dangers currently faced.

My prayer is that as you continue to read, study, and pray your way through the rest of this book you will become better equipped to pray around those issues that deal with the Lord's return. If you are not yet passionately eager for and longing for Jesus' appearing, it is time to pray that you will become so. Here is my prayer for you today.

PRAYER

Lord, how I love the fact that You allow us all to experience Your presence in a wonderful way, even though we find ourselves still in the flesh and waiting for the fullness of our redemption. But You have made us to be those who will live forever with You. I can't wait to see You face-to-face. May each person who reads this prayer be filled by Your Holy Spirit with an overwhelming desire to see Your glorious appearing. Pour out Your love upon us. Give us all a passionate love and desire for You that surpasses anything that is in this world. May we find ourselves lining up with Your Word and looking forward to Your appearing with great joy and expectation.

QUESTIONS FOR REFLECTION OR DISCUSSION

1. Is there something about the second coming of Jesus that scares you? If so, what? What passages of Scripture would help alleviate that fear?

2. The author suggested three reasons why many Christians do not look forward to the return of Jesus. What other reasons can you suggest?

3. What things could you do over the next few days and weeks that would cause you to more greatly look forward to the return of Jesus?

Chapter Two

PRAYING ABOUT THE NEWS

I 've shared before how my father, in a sense, first opened the door for me to look at world events as connected with God's Word and His purposes unfolding on planet Earth. It has been a joy and an exciting adventure to watch the news on television or read a newspaper and see happenings as something more than a depiction of events that are out of my control. Instead, the very things taking place around us are an indication that God is indeed in control and has put in His Word some amazing details of what is about to happen.

All too often, Christians feel powerless and at the mercy of a very big world. Watching or reading of news events can feel like an exercise in futility and even worse, bring a sense of anxiety and worry into our lives. One way to deal with this is to shut yourself off from the world. Turn off the television news and unsubscribe to your daily newspaper. Doing so may provide temporary relief but certainly does nothing to change the situation.

There is a better way. It involves a commitment to change your world through prayer. It happens as you see God's commitment to prayer as a change agent. You begin to see yourself as a player on the world stage. Rather than passively watching and worrying, or ignoring and hiding, you begin to take significant action to bring God's power to bear on situations going on in the world. You pray!

WATCHING POLITICAL EVENTS UNFOLD

The Bible is filled with examples of God's people watching political and national events unfold around them, and then intervening through prayer to bring change. Sometimes a national leader, such as King Asa or King Jehoshaphat of Judah, prayed when faced with a crisis. In both cases, a military attack against the nation was overcome by the prayer of a godly leader.

Sometimes, though, the intervention of God comes through the prayers of more common people, such as Anna and Simeon in the New Testament. These two faithful prayer warriors were watching the signs of the times and understanding the prophetic Old Testament Scriptures that pointed to the soon appearing of the Messiah. God used their prayers to prepare for Messiah's coming in ways that we won't understand until heaven.

A group of ordinary believers crowded into a house in Jerusalem when they heard that the apostle Peter had been arrested and was chained to a prison wall. What a different twist world history would have taken without the powerful leadership of Peter! But God heard the prayers of these little-known believers and sent an angel to release Peter, allowing him to continue helping shape and lead the fledgling church for years.

Throughout church history, God has used the prayers of believers to change the flow of events and alter what might have been. One of the more dramatic instances of this occurred during World War II and involved the small group of intercessors that gathered in Great

Britain under the leadership of Rees Howells. Again and again, God led them to pray over particular battles and situations, many of which they could not have known about through their natural senses. In numerous situations, the Lord used their prayers to ensure victory and change human history.

Obviously, in cases like this, the prayers by themselves did not bring about victory. Men and women in dangerous places fought fierce battles and some paid the ultimate price. But the prayers of Rees Howells and his band of intercessors brought the power of God into the battles and altered history. For further reading on this amazing story, I recommend Norman Grubb's book, *Rees Howells: Intercessor.*

Most of us don't feel like world changers. We're just trying to get through to the end of the week. But God has provided an amazing opportunity for us to join with Him in intercession and see His power bring transformation. Making the most of this opportunity will take a change of attitude and a different way of responding to the news.

Changing our attitude is probably the most difficult. That's why I've spent the time I have to point out that God has always used people's prayers to bring about changes in world events. If we believe God, then our attitude will begin to shift from passivity to action. Rather than sitting and complaining about things as we watch the news or read the newspaper, we will begin to pray to bring about change. A changed attitude—agreeing with God that someone ought to do something and that He (God) is probably the best someone—will bring us into serious prayer.

That changed attitude will cause us to redeem the time we are using to become aware of world and national events. We begin to approach the evening news or morning newspaper as serious times of prayer. Instead of passive intake, we move into aggressive inter-vention. I call it prayer!

PRACTICAL WAYS TO PRAY

Let's talk about some practical ways to pray about the news. First of all, decide to become mentally and spiritually prepared and involved. Very intentional praying is required. It doesn't happen accidentally. We don't just sit down to watch a news show and in the midst of a particular segment suddenly remember or decide to pray. This is not bad, but it is so irregular. Make a decision to sit down and watch the news as a prayer event. It will change everything about your experience.

Second, ask the Lord to guide you as you pray. There are so many times we respond to events by telling God what He should do. You'd think we would have learned that He really isn't looking for our advice. He is, however, looking for our cooperation in releasing His power into situations. Many times the best question we can ask is, "God, what are You doing in this situation?" Then follow that up by asking, "God, what do You want to do?" Then pray with God's heart about what you are seeing.

Third, watch the news with God. Invite Him into the experience with you. Ask Him to allow you to see things from His perspective. Things that didn't formerly upset you may cause you to weep in sor-row. Other things that used to make you angry now may become side issues. His ways are so far beyond ours!

Fourth, bring your journal to your prayer time. By your prayer time, I'm talking about your time of watching the news or reading the newspaper. Journal what you are praying about. Write down insights the Lord provides over situations you are watching.

Fifth, ask the Lord if there are any actions for you to take as a result of what you saw and prayed. Prayer is always the first step but rarely the last. You may need to write a letter to someone involved in a news story. You might be called to give money to someone or something. There might be action steps for your family, especially as it relates to preparation for difficult days ahead. The Lord may direct you to change where your money is invested. He may even call you to move from one city (or nation) to another. Prayerful watching can help prepare you to be a more effective servant in the Lord's hands.

Sixth, bring your Bible with you when you watch the news or read the newspaper. As you pay closer attention to the prophetic Word of God, you will often be reminded of a passage of Scripture as you are watching or reading. Having your Bible with you will help you look up passages and verify that you are, in fact, literally living the Bible as you see things happen right before your eyes.

I will never forget June 6, 1967. I was almost fourteen years old. Dad was watching television news and called me in to watch with him. Pointing to the news that Israeli forces had just taken posses-sion of the Temple Mount and the rest of Jerusalem, he said, "You've just seen a fulfillment of Bible prophecy. Jesus said that Jerusalem would be trampled on by the Gentiles until the time of the Gentiles was fulfilled. Now you've seen it with your own eyes." That was a powerful demonstration for me of how to view the news through biblical eyes. In the very near future, you will see many such things if you are watching.

That brings me to another practical idea: Bring others to your prayer meeting. If you live with family, invite them to join you as you pray about the news. What a wonderful way to teach your children or spouse how to join their prayers to God's purposes. Perhaps you could have a weekly time when you invite friends to your home to pray about the news with you. What dramatic times of intercession might be unleashed as we pray together over the great events of our day!

PRAYER

Father, give me eyes to see what is happening around me. Help me to see things from Your perspective. I choose to use times of exposure to news from around the world as valuable times of intercession. Help me to be disciplined in praying as I watch and read. Show me how You would have me pray. Thank You for allowing me to be a part of what You are doing in the world today.

QUESTIONS FOR REFLECTION AND DISCUSSION

1. Have you ever tried to pray regularly as you watched or read the news? Was it easy or hard for you? Why?

2. Can you think of biblical examples where individuals prayed and national or world events changed? What incidents come to mind?

3. Has there been a particular news event that prompted you to pray? What about that event caused you to pray?

Chapter Three

PRAYER AND END-TIMES WARFARE

There is no doubt that we live in an age of terror. The threat of terrorism affects us every time we go to an airport or cast a vote. It affects the policies of nations and the daily lives of individuals. Nations are mobilizing to face this increasingly dangerous threat.

What is the church's response to terrorism? It certainly affects us. In some places, the church has been the target of terror attacks. In order for the church to fully engage this threat, we must see the spiritual aspect of what is happening. Read the following passage of Scripture from Isaiah, and see whether or not it is able to be applied to terrorists today.

> Their deeds are evil deeds, and acts of violence are in their hands. Their feet rush into sin; they are swift to shed innocent blood. Their thoughts are evil thoughts; ruin and destruction mark their ways. The way of peace they do not know; there is no justice in their paths. They have turned them into crooked roads; no one who walks in them will know peace. (Isaiah 59:6–8)

Terrorism is not merely a matter of physical struggle. It is a spiritual battle as well. This type of blind violence is indicative of Satan's handiwork. Jesus said of Satan in John chapters 8 and 10 that he is a liar, a thief, and a murderer. His intent is to steal, kill, and destroy. In Revelation chapter 12, the devil is described as one who leads the whole world astray. He is filled with fury because he knows his time is short.

While in Thailand recently, I heard British prayer leader Brian Mills say, "Satan undermines truth, is full of self-importance, has revealed that children are a legitimate target, is vehemently anti-Jewish and anti-Christian, and seeks to interrupt our communication with God and with one another. In short, Satan is a terrorist! We see a spirit of violence, intrinsic within Islam, being turned outwards."

Because the struggle against terrorism is one aspect of the cosmic war between the kingdom of God and the kingdom of the prince of this world, Christians must step to the forefront of the battle. As in all of our warfare, prayer becomes a major weapon in our arsenal.

As I mentioned before, Rees Howells and a group of English intercessors gathered regularly to watch and pray over the major battles and events of World War II. There were numerous occasions where God showed them what must happen in advance of the events themselves. These faithful intercessors prayed strategic prayers that changed the direction of military events.

It is time today, in our current warfare against terrorism, for the watchmen to again rise up. The Old Testament uses the term "watchmen" on several occasions to define and describe the actions of intercessors such as Rees Howells and those who prayed with him. The prophet Isaiah cries out, "I have posted watchmen on

your walls, O Jerusalem; they will never be silent day or night"
(Isaiah 62:6a).

What do watchmen do?

- They are to watch and pray.
- They are to be on guard constantly and so provide protection.
"Arise, cry out in the night, as the watches of the night begin"
(Lamentations 2:19).
- They are to listen. Jeremiah 6:17 says, "I appointed watchmen
over you and said, 'Listen to the sound of the trumpet.'"
- They are to warn. "Son of man, I have made you a watchman
for the house of Israel; so hear the word I speak and give
them warning from me" (Ezekiel 3:17).
- They are to call on the Lord. "I have posted watchmen on
your walls. . . . You who call on the LORD, give yourselves
no rest" (Isaiah 62:6).

God has called His people to be watchmen. We are not to be
passive observers or victims in the war against terror. We are to
watch and pray. When we read newspapers, we pray. As we watch
the news, we pray.

In this kind of battlefield mentality, our prayers must be militant
as well. We must pray for a hedge of protection for those on the front
line of battle. We ask God to protect the innocent. It is at times like
this that we ask the Lord of the hosts of heaven to move out against
the enemies of God. We pray that the purposes of God would be
fulfilled in the midst of these threats.

Every nation needs watchmen. God is calling us to the walls to
watch and pray. Our prayers will make the difference in the fight

against terrorism. In the darkness of our current situation, God is calling His people to be light. Through our watchful prayer, we release the powerful light of Christ into the battle. Truly, the battle is the Lord's: "This is what the LORD says to you: 'Do not be afraid or discouraged because of this vast army. For the battle is not yours, but God's'" (2 Chronicles 20:15).

A WATCHMAN'S STORY

The young watchman stood silently at his post on the wall. The cool Judean night caused an involuntary shiver. It had been a quiet evening. A few latecomers were allowed through the pedestrian gate, but nothing else. It was almost time for his shift to end when his eyes caught a glimpse of something glowing over the nearest hill to the north. Peering into the darkness, the watchman confirmed that something was amiss not too far from the city. It could be a movement of enemy troops with their torches betraying their position. Of course, it could just be the campfire of travelers, but why now in the middle of the night?

Whatever it was, the young watchman's orders were clear. He was to sound the alarm. Raising the trumpet to his lips, he sounded the three short blasts that would bring his superiors to the wall. Within minutes, the quiet sentry post was filled with soldiers. An armed scouting party was sent to the general area of the fire. The glow from beyond the hill died down and soon the soldiers returned. A shepherd's hut had caught fire when a gust of wind across the sleeping shepherd's coals had ignited the thatch.

Though the fire was not a danger to the city, the watchman was commended by his commanding officer for his sharp eyes. It could easily have been a threat that would have been stopped by the watchful eyes of the young man. This was the very reason why the watchmen were in place.

WATCHMEN OF TODAY

There is a movement of prayer taking place all over the planet that is firmly rooted in Scripture. It is the call of God to His people to take their places on the wall as watchmen. Whether we look to the Old Testament or the New, we find that God is calling us to watch and pray.

Our modern culture does not readily identify with the ancient concept of watchmen on the walls. To accept the Lord's call to this great movement of prayer then, we will need to train ourselves in what it means to be a part of this great company of the "alert." The Isaiah 62 passage, quoted earlier, helps us greatly in this task.

It is clear that the job of a watchman is a continual commitment. It is not sporadic or dependent upon our feelings. Because of the life-or-death nature and constancy of the watchman's task, it is an assignment for the many, not just the one. Believers working in tandem, sharing shifts of prayer, will be the most effective. Isaiah 62:6–7 describes an intensity that must be shared, day and night, never silent, and never stopped: "give yourselves no rest." Only groups of committed believers who band together in watchful prayer will be able to stay at their post.

Notice also in Scripture that it is God who posts the watchmen. This is a divine assignment, not just the latest prayer fad. To stand on the wall as a watchman, stationed there by the Lord Himself, is a great privilege. We need to receive and obey such a call with gratitude and humility.

Perhaps the overwhelming characteristic of watchman prayer is that it is to be done with open eyes. This does not necessarily imply physical eyes, although it certainly can, but our spiritual eyes must be held wide open. We are to watch and pray.

What is it we are looking for as we pray? I would suggest that we first look for an enemy attack. Certainly in Old Testament times, this sort of defensive watchfulness was at the heart of the task. The watchman on the wall was always on the alert for any attempt of an enemy to attack or infiltrate the city. Too many times, the walls of the church and of our cities today are open to attack because of a lack of watchfulness. In 2 Corinthians 2:11, Paul wrote that we are "not unaware" of the schemes of the enemy. Unless praying watchmen are on duty, we too often find ourselves painfully unaware of the attempts of the enemy to disrupt and destroy.

On the opposite end of matter, I believe that the watchmen are also to keep their eyes open to see and discern moves of God. All too often we miss out on what God is doing because we are not paying attention. The watcher should always be asking, "Lord, what are You doing in our church or city this day? Is there something You are calling Your people to do in cooperation with what You are doing?" How much more effective we would be if, instead of starting our own projects for God, we found ourselves acting alongside a current move of God!

The other area for watchfulness is discerning the needs of the people of God. A watchman on the wall in the Old Testament would often see human needs and be able to send someone to meet those needs. Is there someone among you who is prayerfully watching the people of God to see who is hurting or who is in need? We often talk about shepherding the flock of God. What greater way to shepherd than continually to watch in prayer over the sheep the Lord loves?

What will be the results of watchmen prayers? According to Isaiah, we will see the firm establishment of the kingdom of God. The prophet speaks of the establishment of Jerusalem, the dwelling place of God among His people. In both the Old and the New Covenant, Jerusalem represents God among man. Jesus' main message was the coming kingdom, present in Him. Emmanuel, God with us!

Another result of this powerful prayer movement will be that the glory of God will be seen among the nations. As we watch and pray, we find ourselves lining up with the prophet Habakkuk and crying out for the glory of God to cover the earth "as the waters cover the sea" (Habakkuk 2:14). Prayer warriors, it is time to ascend the wall of your city and begin to fulfill your calling as watchmen of God.

PRAYER

O God, help me to watch and pray. Keep my eyes focused on You. Show me others I can pray with over the condition of our nation and the world. Give me insight into the spiritual battles that erupt into acts of terror and violence and lead me into Spirit-led times of intercession that release Your power into these situations.

QUESTIONS FOR REFLECTION AND DISCUSSION

1. Do you worry about terrorism? Do you know anyone who has been directly affected by terrorism? If so, think about or share what happened.

2. Have you ever viewed yourself as a watchman of prayer? How do you think you could move into this ministry of prayer?

3. What are some kingdom-minded things you can pray over the

conflicts and wars in our world? What Scripture passages can you pray for these situations?

Chapter Four

WATCH AND PRAY

As soon as we begin to talk about the Second Coming of Jesus, it seems as though most Christians want to talk of nothing but speculation:

- Will the temple be rebuilt? Where?
- Will the Rapture happen before, in the midst of, or after the Tribulation?
- Will there be a Great Tribulation?
- Which world leader is the Antichrist?

After examining Scripture about the Second Coming, you will find that the focus is not on trying to figure out the details in advance, but rather on the response of the Christian to the imminent return of Christ. Look how Jesus commands us to respond to indications of the nearness of His return in the following passages.

Matthew 24
- "Watch out that no one deceives you" (verse 4).
- "See to it that you are not alarmed" (verse 6).
- Stand "firm to the end" (verse 13).

- "Keep watch" (verse 42).

Mark 13

- "Watch out that no one deceives you" (verse 5).
- "Do not be alarmed" (verse 7).
- "Be on your guard" (verse 9).
- "Do not worry" (verse 11).
- Stand "firm to the end" (verse 13).
- "Be on your guard" (verse 23).
- "Be on your guard! Be alert!" (verse 33).
- "Keep watch" (verse 35).
- "Watch!" (verse 37).

Luke 21

- "Watch out that you are not deceived" (verse 8).
- "Do not be frightened" (verse 9).
- Stand "firm" (verse 19).
- "Stand up and lift up your heads" (verse 28).
- "Be careful" (verse 34).
- "Be always on the watch, and pray" (verse 36).

This last verse, Luke 21:36, I believe, sums up the biblical response of the Christian to the return of the Lord: "Be always on the watch, and pray." God today appears to be restoring the Watch of the Lord. Christians around the world are beginning to take seriously the command to watch and pray. There are even places where prayer is lifted up continuously.

In his excellent book *The Lost Art of Intercession,* Jim Goll describes the job of a watchman.

The Greek word for "watch" in these verses is *gregoreuo,* and it means "to be vigilant, wake, to be watchful." A watchman on the wall does many things. He carefully watches what is happening and alerts the community when good ambassadors approach the city. The guardsman then will open the gates and lower the bridge so the ambassadors may enter. A watchman also warns the city far in advance when an enemy approaches. He sounds an alarm to awaken the people because he knows "to forewarn them is to alert and arm them." Then they quickly can rally to take their stand on the wall against the enemy before he wrongfully tries to enter the city. (p. 62)

What a powerful picture of the role of the intercessor in God's plans. God has given instructions concerning the watchmen on the walls in Ezekiel 33 and to those who kept watch during the building of Jerusalem's walls during Nehemiah's day. Today, the church is once again being called to the walls of our cities as watchmen.

We have a great historical model of what it means to be watchmen and how that can affect world history. I'm referring to the Moravian prayer watch that began in 1727 and lasted for more than one hundred years. In an article entitled "A Prayer Meeting that Lasted 100 Years," author Leslie K. Tarr gives this astonishing information (see "Prayer Meetings" at www.watchword.org):

FACT: The Moravian community of Hermhut in Saxony, in 1727, commenced an around-the-clock "prayer watch" that continued nonstop for over a hundred years.

FACT: By 1792, 65 years after the commencement of that prayer vigil, the small Moravian community had sent forth 300 missionaries to the ends of the earth.

Could it be that there is some relationship between those two facts? Is fervent intercession a basic component in world evangelization? The answer to both questions is surely an unqualified "yes." That heroic 18th century evangelization thrust of the Moravians has not received the attention it deserves. But even less heralded than their missionary exploits is that hundred-year prayer meeting that sustained the fires of evangelism.

During its first five years of existence the Herrnhut settlement showed few signs of spiritual power. By the beginning of 1727 the community of about three hundred people was wracked by dissension and bickering. An unlikely site for revival! Zinzendorf and others, however, covenanted to pray and labor for revival. On May 12, revival came. Christians were aglow with new life and power, dissension vanished and unbelievers were converted. Looking back to that day and the four glorious months that followed, Count Zinzendorf later recalled: "The whole place represented truly a visible habitation of God among men." A spirit of prayer was immediately evident in the fellowship and continued throughout "that golden summer of 1727," as the Moravians came to designate that period.

On August 27 of that year twenty-four men and twenty-four women covenanted to spend one hour each day in scheduled prayer. Some others enlisted in the "hourly intercession." "For over a hundred years, the members of the Moravian Church all shared in the 'hourly intercession.' At home and abroad, on land and sea, this prayer watch ascended unceasingly to the Lord," stated historian A. J. Lewis.

The church today is increasingly looking to the example of these godly Moravians and their one-hundred-year prayer watch as a model of where God is calling us today. The spiritual deterioration of our world and the church's desperate need for revival demand a response as radical as that practiced by those at Hermhut.

The exciting thing is that it is beginning to happen. Recently, my wife and I spent three days at the International House of Prayer in Kansas City where hundreds gather for prayer and worship that ascends to the Father twenty-four hours a day, seven days a week. God is raising up similar models of unending praise and intercession in cities around the United States. Even individual churches are looking for ways to establish continual prayer.

We're beginning to see prayer not as a quick fix but as a way of life that opens the door for God's power to be poured out upon us. If you are in a city where there is a Watch of the Lord operating, please become a part of that group. If there is no place of continual prayer near you, begin to pray, asking God to raise up those who are willing to take prayer to a whole new level in your church and community. Let's be willing to pay the price to see revival come to our world!

DEVOTION TO PRAYER

"Devote yourselves to prayer, being watchful and thankful" (Colossians 4:2).

Devotion to prayer was one of the marks of the early church. In Acts 2:42, Luke lists four areas of devotion that marked the Jerusalem church: apostles' teaching, fellowship, the breaking of bread, and prayer. The rest of Acts demonstrates its devotion, as a praying church breaks out of Judea and embarks upon its mission to the world.

God's call to His people today is for nothing less than that demonstrated by the first believers. As we depend upon His power through prayer, we establish His kingdom in the lives of men and women everywhere, seeing Christ's kingdom advance among the nations.

In Colossians 4:2, Paul's command for us to be devoted to prayer is sharpened by the phrase "being watchful." Watchful praying is a more intense, more kingdom-focused type of prayer. All too often our prayers can be a reflection of an unfocused, bland faith. We ask little, expect little, and what we do ask for is more about our own desires than the purposes and plans of God.

Watchful praying takes effort. It is an aggressive sort of prayer life, recognizing that life is lived in the midst of a battleground. Watching and praying is a lifestyle focused on seeing the kingdom of Christ advance and knowing that our prayers are a vital part of what God is doing on planet Earth.

To watch and pray first of all means that we watch God. As we draw near in intimacy and see how God is moving, we pick up divine cues from Him as to how we should pray. Scripture speaks much of keeping our eyes on the Lord. Here are some examples:

- "O my Strength, I watch for you; you, O God, are my fortress. . . ." (Psalm 59:9). [my loving God]
- "But as for me, I watch in hope for the LORD, I wait for

God my Savior; my God will hear me" (Micah 7:7).

- "I will stand at my watch and station myself on the ramparts; I will look to see what He will say to me, and what answer I am to give to this complaint" (Habakkuk 2:1).

- "It's like a man going away: He leaves his house and puts his servants in charge, each with his assigned task, and tells the one at the door to keep watch. Therefore keep watch because you do not know when the owner of the house will come back—whether in the evening, or at midnight, or when the rooster crows, or at dawn. If he comes suddenly, do not let him find you sleeping. What I say to you, I say to everyone: 'Watch!'" (Mark 13:34–37).

God's Word also tells us to watch what is happening around us, and sometimes even within us. We are to have an awareness of our surroundings, and what God might be doing in and through them, so that we can pray with greater effectiveness. Here are just a few of the Scriptures that point to this way of watching and praying:

- "Look at the nations and watch—and be utterly amazed. For I am going to do something in your days that you would not believe, even if you were told" (Habakkuk 1:5).

- "Therefore keep watch, because you do not know on what day your Lord will come" (Matthew 24:42).

- "Then he said to them, 'My soul is overwhelmed with sorrow to the point of death. Stay here and keep watch with me.' Going a little farther, he fell with his face to the ground and prayed, 'My Father, if it is possible, may this cup be taken from me. Yet not as I will, but as you will.' Then he returned to his disciples and found them sleeping. 'Could you men not keep watch with me for one hour?' he asked Peter. 'Watch and pray so that you will not fall into temptation. The spirit is willing, but the body is weak'" (Matthew 26:38–41).

- "Only be careful, and watch yourselves closely so that you do not forget the things your eyes have seen or let them slip from your heart as long as you live. Teach them to your children and to their children after them" (Deuteronomy 4:9).

One of the most fascinating aspects of watchful praying is how closely it ties us to the very nature and activity of God Himself. God is a watcher! Again and again in the Bible we read of how He watches over the affairs of both nations and individuals. He calls us to join Him on His watch and to devote ourselves to watch and pray that we might participate with our Lord in His purposes. What an amazing privilege! Carefully consider these Scriptures that point to God on His watch:

- "I am with you and will watch over you wherever you go, and I will bring you back to this land. I will not leave you until I have done what I have promised you" (Genesis 28:15).
- "I will instruct you and teach you in the way you should go; I will counsel you and watch over you" (Psalm 32:8).
- "He rules forever by his power, his eyes watch the nations— let not the rebellious rise up against him" (Psalm 66:7).
- "The LORD will keep you from all harm—he will watch

over your life; the LORD will watch over your coming and going both now and forevermore" (Psalm 121:7–8).

- "The eyes of the LORD are everywhere, keeping watch on the wicked and the good" (Proverbs 15:3).

Would you join today with a watching God? He is calling His people to such an intimate place with Him that we begin to see some aspects of what He is seeing as He allows us that privilege. Our watching is for the purpose of praying into our world the purposes and plans of God. How amazing is the grace and calling of God that He would grant us the joy and favor of laboring alongside Him through watchful praying!

PRAYER

Father, I thank You for continually watching over me. I commit myself now to joining You on Your watch. Show me more and more of Your purposes that I may join my prayers with Your desires. Wake me in the middle of the night to pray whenever You desire. Help me to join with others in day and night prayer that we might see Your glory cover the earth as the waters cover the sea.

QUESTIONS FOR REFLECTION AND DISCUSSION

1. Have you ever been part of an extended-length group prayer gathering such as a twenty-four-hour prayer watch? Was it a good experience? What did you learn from it?

2. Do you sense a special call to prayer from the Lord today? How do you think you can best respond to that?

3. What is a practical way that you can become a prayer watchman? How will that change your current prayer habits?

Chapter Five

PRAYING THROUGH TOUGH TIMES

For many years, Christians have worked on the spiritual disciplines in their lives. Discipline is a very negative word for many people. It can speak of punishment for doing wrong. But the main focus of discipline is learning or training. We train ourselves to accomplish a particular task or ability. Discipline is that training process.

The particular discipline you work on depends upon your goal. If you want to become an Olympic diving champion, you will set for yourself the discipline of practicing your dives many times, every day, for a very long period. It's not necessarily fun, but you do it to achieve a goal.

The ultimate goal for the follower of Christ is to become Christlike. Paul said it this way in Colossians 1:28: "We proclaim him, admonishing and teaching everyone with all wisdom, so that we may present everyone perfect in Christ." A desire for intimacy with Christ is the foundation for everything else in the Christian life. Therefore, the disciplines we put into our lives should be ones intended to help us achieve this goal.

Fasting, solitude, silence, meditation, and prayer are a few of the better known spiritual disciplines that help us move more into a life of intimacy with Christ. There are other disciplines that are sometimes less popular. Perhaps the least popular is the discipline of suffering.

Who would choose the discipline of suffering? Well, Jesus for one. He chose suffering because of His great love for us. Willing to endure suffering for a redemptive purpose, He chose the cross. We must move in the direction of the cross if we are to be intimate with Jesus. Peter said it this way: "To this you were called, because Christ suffered for you, leaving you an example, that you should follow in his steps" (1 Peter 2:21).

The discipline of suffering is not for those who perversely enjoy pain. It is, instead, the response of Christians to existing suffering, both in their own lives and in the lives of others. It is embracing suffering and then using it to help transform us into Christlikeness. In his classic book *Prayer: Finding the Heart's True Home*, Richard Foster calls this discipline the "Prayer of Suffering." He writes,

> In the Prayer of Suffering we leave far behind our needs
> and wants, even our transformation and union with God.
> Here we give to God the various difficulties and trials
> that we face, asking him to use them redemptively. We
> also voluntarily take into ourselves the griefs and sorrows
> of others in order to set them free. (p. 217)

For Foster, the discipline of suffering happens both when we experience suffering or trials in our own lives as well as when we walk with others through their difficulties. Both have the power to transform us, helping us achieve our goal of becoming more like Christ.

We sometimes have nice sounding phrases or platitudes for those going through difficulties. "Into everyone's life a little rain must fall." Or "You've got to learn to take the good with the bad." To be honest, it's going to take more than a quaint saying to help us deal with the tough blows of life. The Christian life is not one of merely enduring suffering, but triumphing through suffering. William Penn's words, and the title of his famous work, are true: *No Cross, No Crown.*

The discipline of suffering is an attitude developed by those who are committed to following Jesus even to the extent of desiring "the fellowship of sharing in his sufferings" (Philippians 3:10). We grow in this as we agree with the apostle Paul that we will be thankful in the midst of all things. It is a mind-set radically different from a society that seeks to remove itself as far as possible from any kind of discomfort or pain.

There is another aspect to this discipline. Foster calls it "voluntarily taking into ourselves the griefs and sorrows of others in order to set them free." This is true intercessory prayer. It is groaning with and for others who are hurting. It is not inserting a brief mention of the suffering of someone else into your prayer list. Instead, the intercessor lingers over the situation, asking God to allow them to understand; yes, even experience the hurt of the other so that true prayer may be released on the hurting one's behalf.

You've perhaps already experienced this in your life. You've gone to comfort or console a friend in the midst of his or her pain and instead of words you found yourself in tears. Oh, you didn't think it was prayer, but God heard your tears, perhaps much more than your words. You identified with your friend's hurt and you became, in that moment, one whom God could use to bring healing.

I refer again to Richard Foster to bring balance to this teaching:

We need not continue shouldering the burdens of others, but rather we release them into the arms of the Father. Without this releasing the burdens will become too much for us, and depression will set in. Besides, it is not necessary. Our task in reality is a small one: to hold the agony of others just long enough for them to let go of it for themselves. Then together we can give all things over to God. (p. 224)

We live in a hurting world. From the small frustrations of everyday life to major tragedies, we all experience varying degrees of pain and suffering. The question is, "How will we handle these difficulties?" Those who follow Jesus will follow Him to the cross. Suffering becomes a part of the Christian life that allows us to draw even nearer to our Lord. This triumphant lifestyle in the midst of this world's suffering allows us to draw near to those who are hurting and bring them in prayer to the Savior's healing hand. Jesus tells us very clearly, "In this world you will have trouble." But He doesn't leave it there. He continues on to say, "But take heart! I have overcome the world" (John 16:33).

INCREASING SORROWS

Our world is obviously in a time of increasing sorrows and difficulties. What will be our reaction as the people of God? In a self-centered and self-absorbed culture, sufferings and difficulties are to be avoided at all costs. When tough times do impact our culture, the tendency is to run from them, complain about them, or sink into depression. The church is not immune from this pervasive attitude.

As we approach the end of days, it will be absolutely essential for the church to embrace wholeheartedly the spiritual discipline of suffering. Tough times are coming! Paul wrote to Timothy and warned, "There will be terrible times in the last days" (2 Timothy 3:1). Jesus said graphically, "If those days had not been cut short, no one would survive" (Matthew 24:22).

In spite of clear warnings in Scripture, the modern church moves ahead with next to no preparation for these tough times in the days to come. It is time for clear teaching on endurance, suffering, and overcoming prayer. A prepared and prayed-up church will be a triumphant church, even in the midst of troubled times.

At least part of our problem is a theological one. Many, perhaps even a majority, of the church today hold to a pretribulation rapture view of the end times. They believe that before the seven years of the Great Tribulation, the church will be removed (raptured) to be with the Lord. This is the viewpoint of the popular *Left Behind* series of novels, which reflect the teachings of author Tim LaHaye.

I respect the scholarship and integrity of men like LaHaye and many others who hold to this pretribulation rapture position. Without weighing in on the accuracy of the position, I simply want to point out the potential danger of the church counting on missing the tribulation, and then perhaps having to face great difficulties without adequate preparation if that view is wrong.

Even if the Rapture takes place before the Great Tribulation, there will be (and are, in fact, today) terrible times that the church must face. We must not allow an escapist mentality to rule us. "Don't worry about tough times; the Rapture is coming, and we won't have to deal with it." I fear that the church will not accept its responsibility to pray and minister in the power of the Holy Spirit through the times of crisis that are upon us.

Perhaps the greatest asset we can have when approaching a correct understanding of events leading up to the Lord's return is humility. I doubt seriously that any of us have a completely accurate viewpoint. We must respect each other's teaching and hold to our own loosely. This is not to say that we cannot or should not teach with as great a degree of accuracy as we can. But godly Christians disagree and we must do so without anger or division.

To the many who believe that Christians will miss the last seven years of human history because they will be taken away by the Lord in the Rapture, I say, "Praise God!" But just in case that timing is inaccurate, be prepared to move through those days in powerful prayer, depending on the power of God to use us to accomplish His purposes through our intercessions. It is not the wrath of God we would face in those days; we are protected from that. If we are here through those days, it is the wrath of Satan that we face, though not without the strength of the Lord as our shield.

PRAYER

Lord, we long for Your appearing. As the nations and the very earth itself convulses in anticipation, please give us Your lasting peace in the midst of troubling times. Help me to endure any hardship for Your sake. I want to be like You, Lord Jesus, as You endured the cross for the joy set before You. May You be my strength and my shield in every situation.

QUESTIONS FOR REFLECTION AND DISCUSSION

1. Do you believe that things will get difficult before the Lord's return? Do you feel spiritually equipped to handle that if it occurs during your lifetime? If not, what will you do to change that feeling?

2. Consider one of the painful or difficult times of your life? How did the Lord bring you through that? Have you been able to see positive effects in your life from that experience?

3. Have you experienced the intercessions of a friend who "bore your burden" in prayer during a difficult time? Have you been able to do that for another? How do you think you can grow in that area of ministry?

Chapter Six

PRAYER AND THE END-TIME REVIVAL

Theories abound as to what must happen before Jesus returns to earth. A common belief from the past, though still present to some degree today, suggests that the church will continue to grow and expand its influence, transforming society till the thousand years of Christ's rule (the millennium) is established on the earth. Dominant two centuries ago, this postmillennial belief system is evident in Dominion theology today, but is relatively small in number of adherents.

Larger numbers of people hold to a more symbolic understanding of the millennium as occurring throughout church history, with Satan being bound through the preaching of the gospel. For these amillennialists, the events immediately preceding the return of Jesus are often considered to be less than transparent. The Second Coming is a bit more of a complete surprise, with little needed in the way of looking for signs of His appearing.

The dominant theology today among evangelicals pictures a world getting much worse before the return of Jesus, with a final segment of time called the Great Tribulation, followed by the triumphant return of Jesus and His rule over the earth for one thousand years. This premillennial view has a number of variants, including disagreement over whether or not Christians are supernaturally removed (the Rapture) before, during, or after the times of tribulation.

With the exception of the smallest of the groups, the postmillennialists, virtually all Christians believe that conditions will worsen on this planet before the second coming of Christ. This often leads to a defeatist mind-set that says, "Since things are going to get worse and worse, we just need to barricade ourselves against a world gone bad and getting worse." There is typically no expectation of anything significantly good happening before the end.

Regardless of your view of the millennium, I believe the Scriptures teach of a great end-time revival that will prepare the church for the coming of her Lord. It is not clearly stated as such in any one place, but a case can be built from several different passages:

- After healing the crippled beggar in Jerusalem, Peter said, "Repent, then, and turn to God, so that your sins may be wiped out, that times of refreshing may come from the Lord, and that he may send the Christ, who has been appointed for you—even Jesus. He must remain in heaven until the time comes for God to restore everything, as he promised long ago through his holy prophets" (Acts 3:19–21).
- "The harvest is the end of the age" (Matthew 13:39).
- "Let us rejoice and be glad and give him glory! For the wedding of the Lamb has come, and his bride has made herself ready. Fine linen, bright and clean, was given her to wear. (Fine linen stands for the righteous acts of the saints.)" (Revelation 19:7–8).

"Times of refreshing" from the Lord before He comes to restore everything according to ancient prophecies seems to indicate a reviving move of God. A great harvest of souls would go hand in hand with a sweeping revival of the church before Jesus' return. The readiness of the bride of Christ through the righteous acts of the saints seems to indicate a purifying work of God that the church has yet to experience. All of this leads me and many others to believe and pray toward another great awakening before the second coming of Jesus.

And what of those passages of scripture that speak of terrible days? This will be a revival in the midst of spiritual warfare. As Satan becomes aware that his time is short and pours out his fury, so the forces of God respond in the power of the Holy Spirit. God does not leave us helpless and defenseless against the attacks of the enemy. A great reviving move of the Spirit of God enables the church not only to stand but also to prevail in the midst of darkness.

What is this thing called revival? I believe that revival is the church waking up to the presence of Jesus in her midst. It is nothing more and nothing less than you and I beginning to experience what we already know theologically and intellectually. You believe that Jesus is with you. Why? Because He said He would be. You don't necessarily believe it because you feel Him, but just because Jesus said it. He said that where two or three are gathered together there am I in your midst (Matthew 18:20). You also have to believe Colossians 1:27: "Christ in you, the hope of glory."

We believe that Jesus is present when we gather as the church, but we don't act that way on our typical day of worship. You know why I know your church needs revival? The reason I know your church needs revival is because when church services ended last week, you went home.

What would happen if Jesus was there? Let's just suppose Jesus was there. Would you be looking at your watch? Would you be eager to leave? One of the characteristics of the great revivals was extended times of worship. They never wanted to end the service. Now obviously people had to leave. They had to take care of physical things, they had jobs that they had to go to, but as soon as they were done they were back because that was where God was. They wanted to be in on the action. They wanted to be where God was. They wanted to experience His presence.

STRANGE OR MYSTICAL

I want to suggest to you that revival is not strange or mystical. It is simply the church waking up to the presence of Christ in her midst. It is almost as though God reaches out and slaps us, and we wake up and realize God is there. That is what revival is. It is God shaking us. It is God waking us up. And we recognize that Jesus really is here.

We are desperate for that in our nation today. I am not in any way a critic of the church. The more I travel the more I fall in love with the church of Jesus Christ. I am seeing so many wonderful things happen. Christians are doing wonderful things in the name of Jesus, acts of love, mercy, and self-sacrifice. It is amazing what is happening today and has been happening for years. We are doing all we know to do. But it isn't working.

Most churches have all kinds of activities. They've tried all kinds of programs. They've given and done everything they know how to do to get the church going and to impact society. In all that has happened in the last fifty years in the church in the United States, are we a more moral and ethical nation because of what the church has been doing? Despite tremendous acts of sacrifice, service, and ministry, it is apparent that the church is going one way and our nation is moving rapidly the opposite way.

In a very real sense, we are at this wonderful point of despair. We are at a wonderful point of hopelessness in which the church is beginning to recognize that we have been doing everything we know how to do and it is not working. It is time for revival. It is time to humble ourselves before God in prayer and ask Him to make Himself known in the midst of His people so that our nation can be saved and our world impacted for Christ.

How does revival come? Any student of revival will tell you that there has never been a revival without a movement of prayer. God always calls His people to prayer in anticipation of revival. I ask you today to get serious about praying for revival. We need to shift our prayer focus to the issues that are close to God's heart, asking especially that His people, His church, would wake up and discover the presence of Jesus in our midst.

When that happens, our lives become different. When Jesus is there, suddenly things that we accepted before are no longer acceptable. Some of the things that go on in our churches and in our society are changed because the Lord is present. That is why in those great revivals in the past there was a bit of emotionalism. Suddenly they came into a church service and there was Jesus. They did not see Him in the flesh, but they had a powerful sense of the presence of Jesus. What do you suppose happens if you come into a church service during a revival and there is a strong sense of the presence of Jesus and you've been sinning all week? When you come into the presence of the awesome holiness of God, suddenly you weep, cry out, and sometimes even fall down before God in repentance.

Heaven-sent revival is our only hope. We don't have answers. We don't know what to do. We don't have any programs in our churches that are changing whole communities and our society. It's just not happening. What we need is God.

How do you pray for revival? Psalm 85:1–6 is a good place to begin: "You showed favor to your land, O LORD; you restored the fortunes of Jacob. You forgave the iniquity of your people and covered all their sins. You set aside all your wrath and turned from your fierce anger. Restore us again, O God our Savior, and put away your displeasure toward us. Will you be angry with us forever? Will you prolong your anger through all generations? Will you not revive us again, that your people may rejoice in you?"

PRAYER

Lord, revive us again; do it again in our day. Lord, this is what You have done in the past, and this is what we ask You to do again in our lives and in our churches. We are desperate for revival. I, personally, am desperate for Your reviving touch and ask for that today in my own life. Wake me up to the reality of Your transforming presence in my life.

QUESTIONS FOR REFLECTION AND DISCUSSION

1. Do you believe that there will be a great revival at the end of days? Why or why not? Do you see any indicators of a coming revival?

2. Have you experienced a personal revival or renewal in your life? What prompted or led you into that experience?

3. Do you regularly pray for revival? Why or why not?

Chapter Seven

PRAYER AND THE TASK OF WORLD EVANGELIZATION

God is doing a new thing today. If you want to be in on what God is doing, you must begin praying with greater passion and intensity. If you want purpose and meaning to life and if you want your life to really count for God and to make a difference in this world, *pray*! Prayer is what God is calling His people to do today as a part of His plan for this world.

God is moving all things toward completion. I don't pretend to know when or how or any of the details that people often get so excited about. But I do know the key to the completion of God's purposes on this planet. It is evangelism. And the key to evangelism is prayer. Let me show this to you through the words of Scripture.

Jesus said, "And this gospel of the kingdom will be preached in all the whole world as a testimony to all nations, and then the end will come" (Matthew 24:14). The gospel is going to be preached to all nations. Jesus said so. If Jesus said it, I firmly believe it will happen. Sometime after the gospel has been preached to the whole world, the end of all things will come. Evangelism is tied to the second coming of Christ. Without delving into issues of dates and times, the question for us today is, "Do we want to be a part of the fulfillment of Jesus' words?"

Jesus ties together prayer and evangelism in Matthew 9:37–38: "Then he said to his disciples, 'The harvest is plentiful but the workers are few. Ask the Lord of the harvest, therefore, to send out workers into his harvest field.'" The instruction of Jesus to His disciples regarding reaching the lost is that it begins with prayer. There is certainly more to do after we have prayed, but evangelism will never be truly effective apart from the biblical beginning place of prayer.

The apostle Paul continues this teaching in his first letter to Timothy: "I urge, then, first of all, that requests, prayers, intercession and thanksgiving be made for everyone—for kings and all those in authority, that we may live peaceful and quiet lives in all godliness and holiness. This is good, and pleases God our Savior, who wants all men to be saved and to come to a knowledge of the truth" (1 Timothy 2:1–4). Notice that Paul urges that prayers be lifted up, because God wants everyone saved. Prayer and evangelism are brought together in a powerful way and linked to the very purposes of God.

Not to be left out, the apostle John shows us in his unique way that prayer and evangelism are inextricably connected. There are two passages of Scripture in Revelation that you may not have noticed before that are exciting in their presentation of prayer and evangelism:

- "Each one had a harp and they were holding golden bowls full of incense, which are the prayers of the saints" (Revelation 5:8b).
- "Another angel, who had a golden censer, came and stood at the altar. He was given much incense to offer, with

the prayers of all the saints, on the golden altar before
the throne. The smoke of the incense, together with the
prayers of the saints, went up before God from the angel's
hand" (Revelation 8:3–4).

After each of these incidents in which the collected prayers of
God's people are poured out before God, angels are loosed upon the
earth to cause events intended to bring people to repentance and
salvation. God uses the prayers of His people to bring about the
establishment of Christ's kingdom.

The second passage above in Revelation comes in the midst of
a half an hour of silence. In an article titled "The Watchword in
World Missions" in the fall 1999 issue of the *International Journal of
Frontier Missions*, authors Jay Gary and Todd Johnson quote Walter
Wink explaining the connection this way:

> Heaven itself falls silent. The heavenly hosts and
> celestial spheres suspend their ceaseless singing so that
> the prayers of the saints on earth can be heard. The seven
> angels of destiny cannot blow the signal of the next
> times to be until an eighth angel gathers these prayers
> and mingles them with incense upon the altar. Silently
> they rise to the nostrils of God.
>
> Human beings have intervened in the heavenly lit-
> urgy. The uninterrupted flow of consequences is dammed
> for a moment. New alternatives become feasible. The
> unexpected becomes suddenly possible, because God's
> people on earth have invoked heaven, the home of the
> possibles and have been heard. What happens next

happens because people prayed. The message is clear: history belongs to the intercessors. (p. 162)

Dick Eastman explained it to me this way: "God's ultimate purpose for mankind, the completion of Christ's bride and the establishing of His eternal Kingdom on earth will result only from the release of the prayers of God's saints."

Graham Kendrick and Chris Robinson wrote the hymn "All Heaven Waits." See if their words call to your heart and stir within you a passion to be a person of prayer:

> All heaven waits with bated breath for saints on earth
>   to pray,
> Majestic angels ready stand with swords of fiery blade.
> Astounding power awaits a word from God's resplendent
>   throne.
> But God awaits our prayer of faith that cries, "Your
>   will be done."

There is a fascinating change taking place in the way the church perceives prayer. From dusty devotions and personal needs, prayer has taken center stage in our attempts to reach the lost. Prayer seems to have become the divine strategy for the completion of the task of world evangelization. Wherever the church is growing the most, you find the church praying the best.

The explosion of prayer evangelism is happening in Korea, in Argentina, in many places in Africa, and it's beginning to happen in North America as well. Christians are creatively bringing together prayer and evangelism in ways that are overcoming both natural and spiritual barriers to Christian conversion.

It's important at the outset to understand that prayer evangelism is not some sort of mystical weirdness where we pray and then sit back and do nothing else. It is, rather, a releasing of God's power through prayer that is focused on overcoming barriers to evangelism and on preparing the soil of an individual's life to receive the gospel. We pray powerful biblical prayers, and then our evangelistic efforts follow with far greater effectiveness.

Paul wrote to Timothy, saying that God wants us to pray, interceding for everyone (1 Timothy 2:1–4). Why? Because God wants everyone saved. The New Testament teaches us much on the power of prayer in evangelism. Somehow the church has lost the connection. My friend Terry Teykl of Renewal Ministries says that sometime after the first century the great divorce occurred—the divorce between prayer and evangelism. Prayer became devotional and liturgical, but not very practical; while evangelism became more and more a matter of human effort or even coercion at times. Fortunately, the New Testament concept is being recovered as prayer and evangelism are once again wedded together.

It's happening in many exciting ways. One preacher in Texas asked his congregation to turn in the names of one hundred people who needed to come to Jesus. Those names were prayed over by a trained team of intercessors, and by the end of the year ninety-two of those people had come to faith in Christ. This type of focused praying by those who have been well trained is central to effective prayer evangelism.

One way of praying for the neighborhoods around your church is an innovative method known as prayerwalking. Christians gather at the church building for a time of prayer and preparation. Then they go in groups of two or three through a particular neighbor-hood, walking up and down the street, praying for each house that God would be at work in each home. They do this quietly, without calling attention to themselves or their prayer subjects, but effec-tively releasing God's power into people's lives. Graham Kendrick and Steve Hawthorne wrote a resource book on the topic entitled *Prayerwalking: Praying Onsite with Insight.*

One minister I spoke with, Dee Duke of Jefferson Baptist Church in Jefferson, Oregon, prays for everyone in his church by name every week. To help him remember who is who, he put all of their pictures on his laptop computer so that he can see their faces as he prays. Oh, did I mention that church attendance has gone from 150 to 1,300, and he still prays for everyone by name every week!

Many churches send cards to homes in their neighborhood, asking if there is anything they can be praying about. They do not ask them to come to church, do not ask for money, do not advertise a special program. They just want to know if there is any way they can pray about what is important to those in the neighborhood. It is not long before such a church attracts people who are looking for a church that cares about them enough to ask and pray.

The power of blending prayer and evangelism is not something that is limited to local churches. Whole groups of churches and large evangelistic outreaches are beginning to see the importance of prayer. Mission organizations are beginning to understand that the key to bringing in the harvest of souls worldwide is prayer.

THE HARVEST

I love the harvest time in the Midwest where I live. It is a great time of the year. When I was the pastor in a rural community, I saw first-hand that the harvest was the most critical time of the year. During those fall months, all the hard work from spring and summer was rewarded as the crops were brought in from the fields.

Harvest was a time of intense labor. Farmers knew they often had just a short period of time when the crops were ready and the weather would cooperate to allow them to bring in the harvest before harsh winter weather began. From early in the morning until late at night, farmers worked hard to assure a successful harvest.

There is another kind of harvest that is happening today. It is a harvest of souls. This spiritual harvest is a critical time, much as the fall harvest of crops. It is also a time of intense work in which the laborers cooperate with the Lord of the harvest to reap a harvest of souls.

"Then he said to his disciples, 'The *harvest* is plentiful but the workers are few. Ask the Lord of the *harvest*, therefore, to send out workers into his *harvest* field'" (Matthew 9:37–38, emphasis added). Jesus refers to a harvest of souls that is ready to be brought in and a lack of willing workers. Many churches can identify with His statement. What we need to emphasize here, however, is the Lord's command to pray. The first job of the church in the midst of harvest is to pray to the Lord of the harvest for an increase in workers.

"'Let both grow together until the *harvest*. At that time I will tell the harvesters: First collect the weeds and tie them in bundles to be burned; then gather the wheat and bring it into my barn.' . . . 'The harvest is the end of the age, and the harvesters are angels'" (Matthew 13:30, 39, emphasis added). This is a fascinating teaching by Jesus concerning those in the church who are not true believers. These weeds will grow alongside the true plants, and in the end the

Lord will sort them out. What a relief it is to know that it is not our responsibility to pull out the weeds from among us. It is also clear in this passage that Jesus says the ultimate harvest will be at the end of the age.

"Do you not say, 'Four months more and then the *harvest*'? I tell you, open your eyes and look at the fields! They are ripe for *harvest*. Even now the reaper draws his wages, even now he harvests the crop for eternal life, so that the sower and the reaper may be glad together. Thus the saying 'One sows and another reaps' is true. I sent you to reap what you have not worked for. Others have done the hard work, and you have reaped the benefits of their labor" (John 4:35–38, emphasis added). Not everyone has the same job description in the kingdom of God. Some plant, some water, and some reap. All of us, though, are to be vitally concerned with a great harvest of souls for God.

"I do not want you to be unaware, brothers, that I planned many times to come to you (but have been prevented from doing so until now) in order that I might have a *harvest* among you, just as I have had among the other Gentiles" (Romans 1:13, emphasis added). The apostle Paul had such a passion for souls. His desire to come to Rome was that he might share in harvesting souls there.

"Let us not become weary in doing good, for at the proper time we will reap a *harvest* if we do not give up" (Galatians 6:9, emphasis added). The harvest comes to those who do not give up. There is nothing easy about the harvest, whether it is physical or spiritual. We need to encourage one another not to become weary in doing good. The harvest is coming!

"Then another angel came out of the temple and called in a loud voice to him who was sitting on the cloud, 'Take your sickle and reap, because the time to reap has come, for the *harvest* of the earth is ripe.' So he who was seated on the cloud swung his sickle over the earth, and the earth was harvested" (Revelation 14:15–16, emphasis added). The ultimate harvest is coming. Jesus is coming for His own. I believe the great harvest is beginning. People from every tribe and tongue and nation are hearing and responding to the good news in our day. It is not a day for drawing back or sleeping.

Let us be those who are not weary in doing good, are filled with a passionate love for Jesus, and are longing for a great harvest of souls to lay at Christ's feet at His appearing.

PRAYER

Lord of the harvest, please send workers into the harvest fields. And please begin with me. Show me how You want me to serve You in finishing the task of world evangelization in my day. Teach me to pray in such a way that souls are drawn to You. I pray that, according to Psalm 2, You would receive Your inheritance of the very ends of the earth.

QUESTIONS FOR REFLECTION AND DISCUSSION

1. Were you aware of anyone praying for you before you became a Christian? Have you prayed for others to accept Christ? What has been the result?

2. Do you believe that we are in the midst of the great end-time harvest? Why or why not?

3. Do you know anyone personally who has a great passion for evangelism? What makes them different from other believers? How do you think this passion can be spread in the church?

Chapter Eight

PRAYING FOR ISRAEL

It is no surprise that Israel is a source of division and contention, both in the world and in the church. It has always been so. For reasons, one could look to the unique geographic place of the nation, a bridge of land between warring empires for millennia. Or the exclusivist monotheism of the Jewish faith that set it apart through the ages. Modern analysts perhaps look to the deep-seated antagonism between Jew and Arab as an outgrowth of tribal hatreds born centuries ago, even reaching back to the children of the patriarch Abraham. Christianity's emergence from the root of Israel has led to a confusion of relationship that has shifted like sand through the years, ranging from love and respect to outright persecution.

Though all of these points are true to some extent, I believe there is a spiritual source, literally a demonic one, which underlies the controversy. From the beginning, the great adversary Satan has hated the Jewish people. They were the ones chosen by God through which the purposes of God were to be carried out on planet Earth. Through the Jewish people God's redemptive plan for mankind was to be enacted, thereby assuring Satan of defeat. The persistence and ferocity of anti-Semitism through the centuries can only be explained by a supernatural force. Satan has tried to destroy the out-working of God's grace by destroying the people upon and through which God would demonstrate His greatest grace.

From Haman to Hitler might be a proper, if chilling, title of a book about the deadly nature of anti-Semitism. In the biblical days of Esther and her uncle Mordecai, the Jews faced an enemy in the person of a Babylonian official named Haman whose desire was to have all the Jews killed. Though Haman perished, the spirit behind his deadly schemes did not. History records again and again how hatred against the Jewish people erupted into violence and persecution. In recent history, the efforts of Hitler and his Nazis to eliminate all European Jews during the Holocaust was such a monstrous act that it is hard to imagine such large-scale murder apart from demonic involvement. Certainly Christians who pray for Israel will want to deal significantly with issues of spiritual warfare on behalf of the Jewish people.

This may be hard for some to believe, but even praying for Israel can be a point of controversy for followers of Christ. The significance of the existence of the modern nation of Israel is a point hotly disputed among Christians. I am guessing that the majority of those who pick up this book, titled as it is, are those who believe that the founding of the nation of Israel in 1948 was an astonishing fulfillment of biblical prophecy and that events surrounding Israel are key to understanding the last days. That is certainly my view! But I have many godly friends who hold firmly to the Word of God who believe differently.

I am not here to convince people of my view, but to present effective ways to pray for Israel. Those who do not see modern Israel as a fulfillment of prophecy may well not have the sense of urgency to pray for Israel, but my encouragement to them is still to pray. At the very least, all Christians can join together in obedience to the biblical admonition in Psalm 122:6 to pray for the peace of Jerusalem.

What does it mean to pray for the peace of Jerusalem? First, I would suggest that a prayer for the peace of Jerusalem is not confined to the city alone, but includes the whole nation of Israel. In Old Testament times, the capital city of Jerusalem represented the entire nation. When times of trouble came, much of the nation came inside the walls of Jerusalem for protection. So, then, how do we pray for Jerusalem (Israel)?

Certainly there is the aspect of protection from war, violence, and terrorism that we would all desire for Israel. While it appears prophetically that there will come a time when God's hand of protection is withdrawn for a while from Jerusalem, until then we are to pray for God's peace. This aspect of peace involves a cessation of hostility and attack. If, in spite of our prayers, it appears that violence still occurs, we can only imagine to what extent there would be unbridled violence without our prayers.

In one way, Jerusalem will never completely know peace until the Prince of Peace comes to reign in the city. When Messiah comes (again), He will establish Jerusalem as the praise of all the earth, the place from which He will reign over the earth. There is, however, a peace that comes to the human heart when Jesus is made Lord of that heart and life. I believe it is essential that we pray for the peace of Christ to come into many hearts in Israel. It is this peace that will comfort and endure, even through times of great trial and tribulation.

On the first Sunday in October of each year, many in the church come together for the International Day of Prayer for the Peace of Jerusalem. If your church has not become involved in this powerful prayer event, check out its website at www.daytopray.com. Praying for the peace of Jerusalem is so much more than a one-day event, but this day of prayer can help ignite your prayers for the rest of the year on Israel's behalf.

Psalm 122:6 says, "Pray for the peace of Jerusalem: 'May those who love you be secure.'" With Israel having a central role politically, religiously, and prophetically in the Middle East, much effective intercession needs to be made on her behalf. In her powerful book *Why Care about Israel,* my friend Sandra Teplinsky gives some great things to pray for Israel:

- For the blessing and strengthening of those in true spiritual authority
- For an outpouring of grace leading to repentance for unsaved Jews and Arabs
- For revival and maturity in the Israeli body of Messiah
- For blessing and wisdom for government authorities and others in spheres of leadership
- For God's sending and sustaining of laborers into Israeli harvest fields, opening the doors for Messianic Jewish *aliyah* (return)
- For believers in the nations to send resources to the Messianic community in Jerusalem and the rest of Israel
- For Jerusalem's (Israel's) protection from enemy attack— physical and spiritual
- For Jerusalem's (Israel's) enemies to be delivered from darkness into light
- For material prosperity despite Israel's economic woes due to war
- For your particular nation's blessing of Israel
- For the nations' recognition of Jerusalem as Israel's eternal capital city

- For protection from the spirit of antichrist
- For the fulfillment of Jerusalem's redemptive purpose on earth as the City of the Great King, a city of peace that blesses the nations
- For the gift of intercessory tears to be shed on her behalf until these things come to pass (p. 226).

I love the balance of these intercessory pleas on behalf of Israel. There is no attempt here to accept everything that the modern State of Israel does as an act endorsed by God. Israel is a secular state that has made many mistakes. Nor is there anything that demonizes the opponents of Israel. Instead, in prayer, we choose to align ourselves with God's redemptive and prophetic purposes that have chosen to use Israel as an important part of what God is doing and going to do on planet Earth.

Praying for Israel ultimately is about asking God to use this tiny nation to bring Him glory and to use the Jewish people to bring about His purposes as He has so many times in the past. God uses our prayers for Israel to advance His kingdom and to bring honor to His son, Israel's largely unrecognized Messiah.

Because your prayers for Israel are such a critical part of God's end-time purposes, they are to become more intense as the time approaches. I believe that the day-and-night prayer movement that began about ten years ago and continues to intensify is, in itself, a sign of the approaching end of days. This 24/7 prayer movement is an act of obedience and fulfillment of the command of Scripture: "You who call on the LORD, give yourselves no rest, and give him no rest till he establishes Jerusalem and makes her the praise of the earth" (Isaiah 62:6b–7).

The ten days of day-and-night prayer in Jerusalem before Pentecost launched the church in its mission two thousand years ago. In the early 1700s, the one-hundred-year, day-and-night prayer meeting of the Moravians began the modern missions movement. I believe the current day-and-night prayer movement will usher in the fulfillment of the mission of the church, the glorious appearing of Christ.

PRAYER

God of Israel, how amazed I am at the way You have brought Your people back into the land of promise. In our day we have watched with our own eyes as You have restored Jerusalem to Your people Israel and, against all odds, have brought into being a nation that many have said could never exist again. Now, Lord, pour out that spirit of grace and supplication upon Jerusalem. May Jesus be recognized as Messiah by His own people. Bring peace to Jerusalem as the Prince of Peace is enthroned upon the hearts of the Jewish people and all who dwell in the land.

QUESTIONS FOR REFLECTION AND DISCUSSION

1. Have you ever considered the opposition to Israel today to be the result of satanic activity? What are some of the indications of that activity that you see?

2. Do you believe that modern Israel is a fulfillment of biblical prophesy? What Scriptures would you use to support your view?

3. How have you been praying for Israel? Have you sensed a greater urgency to be praying for Israel? If so, why do you believe that to be the case?

Chapter Nine

DISCERNING THE TIMES

"**H**e [Jesus] said to the crowd: 'When you see a cloud rising in the west, immediately you say, "It's going to rain," and it does. And when the south wind blows, you say, "It's going to be hot," and it is. Hypocrites! You know how to interpret the appearance of the earth and the sky. How is it that you don't know how to interpret this present time?'" (Luke 12:54–56).

How do we understand the times in which we live? Jesus certainly seems to expect us to have the ability to correctly interpret the general moves of God within a generation. He criticized the religious leaders of His day who, having access to the prophetic Word, still did not understand the coming of the Messiah and all that entailed for them. If they missed it, we must assume that we also can fail to discern the times. It is very possible for Christians to get so caught up in everyday living that we never stop and look at the overarching plans and purposes of God for our day.

How then shall we understand our times? Can we emulate the men of Issachar of whom it was said, they understood the times in which they lived and knew what Israel must do? (1 Chronicles 12:32). We'll discuss more about these men later in this chapter.

In the section below, I share with you some words from men of our own generation as well as the two preceding generations who have looked intently into the Word of God and at our world. (Except where noted, all quotes are taken from www.watchword. org, "Quotes" tab). Their comments are enlightening, encouraging, and challenging. As you read, it will become clear that what God is doing in our day is wrapped around prayer, revival, and finishing the task of world evangelization. May our lives be joined with the grand purposes of God for our times.

> Dr. A. T. Pierson said it well, when he said that no revival has ever come except by that kind (Upper Room) of praying, and (he continued) no revival has continued beyond the continuation of the same kind of praying. It's like a fire—what gets it started is what it takes to keep it burning.—Armin Gesswein

> After studying prayer and spiritual awakenings for 60 years I've reached this conclusion . . . whenever God is ready to do something new with His people, He always sets them praying.—Dr. Edwin Orr

> Without a doubt, the major opportunity before us is the potential of a historic revival akin to the first great awakening. . . . The encouraging 'sign' of an impending awakening is the grass-roots prayer movement God is raising up. . . .—Paul Cedar, Chairman of the Mission America Coalition (personal communication)

> Never before in living memory has prayer been rising so rapidly on the agenda of Christian leaders across our nation.

Is the great revival on the way?—C. Peter Wagner

When people sense the Lord is near, they also want to talk with Him. Revival and prayer always go together.— David Mains

When God is about to give His people the expected good, He pours out a Spirit of prayer, and it is a good sign that He is coming toward them in mercy. Then when you see the expected end approaching, *then you shall call upon Me*" (Jeremiah 29:11–12). Note, promises are given not to supersede, but to quicken and encourage prayer: and when deliverance is coming we must by prayer go forth to meet it. When Daniel understood the 70 years were near expiring, then he set his face with more fervency than ever to seek the Lord (Daniel 9:2–3).—Matthew Henry

When prayers and strong pleas for revival are made to God both day and night; when the children of God find they can no longer tolerate the absence of revival blessings; when extraordinary seeking of an extraordinary outpouring becomes extraordinarily earnest; and when the burden of prayer for revival becomes almost unbearable, then let praying hearts take courage, for the Spirit of God who is the spirit of revival has brought His people to this place for a purpose.—Richard Owen Roberts

It's not like an earthquake. It's more like being lifted by the tide, a surging tide of God's grace. Across the world, the new decade is marked by the emergence of city-wide prayer meetings. Some of the largest pastoral prayer meetings in United States history have recently taken place. . . . What is God up to? We can only wonder at His tactics, but His motives are clear enough. He loves us. He has not abandoned our generation. He governs in the affairs of people and nations, and He is setting the stage for harvest.—John Dawson

There have been revivals without much preaching, but there has never been a mighty revival without mighty prayer.—R. A. Torrey

Once again, today God has raised up a multitude who are willing to pay the price both by praying and by preaching, so that the Church might encounter the full panorama of who Christ is. And to the extent that they succeed—to the degree God restores in us an 'abounding hope by the power of the Holy Spirit,' and does so for the Church worldwide—to that degree we will experience a true world revival.—David Bryant

The revival we seek is bearing down on top of us. It will be nothing less than a wide-spread *Christ-awakening movement,* in which God's Spirit uses God's Word to re-convert God's people back to God's Son for ALL that He is.—David Bryant

We live in exciting times for those who belong to the Lord

Jesus. As we look both to the Word and the world in which we live, we can join with the Lord in His work of intercession, revival, and drawing people to Himself. Our prayers will become pleadings for the fulfillment of Habakkuk 2:14: "For the earth will be filled with the knowledge of the glory of the LORD, as the waters cover the sea."

Often when Christians talk about "understanding the times" they assume that we are focusing on prophecies relating to the second coming of Christ. As much as I love studying these kinds of prophecies, they only present a limited scope of what God intends for us to be aware of in our culture and throughout the world. "Understanding the times" is a mind-set and a lifestyle that includes but is not limited to issues relating to the second coming of Christ.

There was an amazing group of people in the Old Testament who lived that kind of lifestyle. They are called in Scripture the "men of Issachar." First Chronicles 12:32 says that these men "understood the times and knew what Israel should do." I believe God is raising up a new generation of this kind of spiritually sensitive, discerning people today.

Biblically speaking, true understanding comes from the fear of God. When we place ourselves before the Lord in awe of who He is and surrender our lives to His lordship, we begin to gain a more accurate understanding of what is happening, not only in our own lives but also in the world around us. As the Spirit of God permeates our lives, we gain an increased awareness of His perspective on events. We no longer look at things around us from the limited perception of our own experiences, but we are able to discern matters from the Lord's viewpoint.

Practically speaking, we will still struggle most of the time to separate our own understanding from the Lord's. We rarely live up to our spiritual potential. Our own background and experiences so often color our viewpoint. But the good news is that there is something more available to us. God's perspective is accessible to us as we depend upon Him through prayer and the Word of God.

Many times we do not understand the times in which we live because we have not asked the Lord what He thinks. Scripture is clear: We do not have because we do not ask (James 4:2). The first step for many of us is to pray this simple prayer: "Lord, please help me to understand the times in which I live. May I not be dependent upon others' opinions but always seek after Your accurate perspective on what is happening in my world."

Though God certainly can demonstrate His perspective to us without any sort of human input, my strong suggestion is that He works more often through knowledge than lack of knowledge. By this I mean we will be more likely to gain clarity about what God thinks if we are carefully and closely watching what is already happening in the world. When a working knowledge of world or national events is wed with the Spirit of God, the result is always more understanding.

Rather than watching the news or reading the newspaper and shaking your head over bad events, why not add a prayer for discernment to your watching and reading? As world events unfold, instead of submitting to despair or anger, seek the Lord's insight over what is occurring. The result will be an understanding of the times in which we live.

The biblical text, however, does not end with the men of Issachar merely understanding the times. They also knew what Israel should do. This adds wisdom to knowledge. Knowing information is one thing. Having the wisdom to know what to do with that knowledge is immensely valuable.

We live in troubled times when there is little understanding of the times. There is probably even less wisdom to know how to deal with those times. How should the people of God live in these days? What sort of direction should the church take in the midst of the confusion of our time? If we, as the people of God, do not even know who we are or where we are going, how can we speak with a strong prophetic voice to our society?

The teachers among the ancient tribe of Issachar must have been doing something right. From the context we know that it was not just one or two leaders who had this understanding. There had to have been good teaching and mentoring for years in order to prepare the men of Issachar for their particular time of crisis. Scripture mentions that eighteen thousand men and their two hundred chiefs all had some understanding of the times and were led to take the steps of action that were appropriate for the people of God.

How we need men and women like this today! We need mentors and spiritually strong leaders who will spend time in the Word of God to know His heart and will then pay attention to what is happening around them. These are the ones who can lead the church into the action necessary to advance Christ's kingdom.

PRAYER

Father, would You raise up people in our midst like the men of Issachar who will understand our times and know what the people of God should do? Help me to be one of them! Give me an understanding that comes from You. Combine knowledge and wisdom within me so that avenues of service and obedience open before me. Raise up an army, Lord, of those who hear clearly from You, that they may raise the clarion call to the people of God in this day!

QUESTIONS FOR REFLECTION AND DISCUSSION

1. Do you have someone in your life whom you believe is discerning of the times in which we live? If not, where might you find someone who can help mentor you in the spiritual understanding of our day?

2. What do you believe God is doing in the world today?

3. Did one of the quotes from the first part of this chapter speak to your heart? Which one and why?

Chapter Ten

IS THE BRIDE READY?

As a minister of the gospel, I have officiated at many weddings. There are so many details to be attended to for a wedding to take place: Guests must be seated, candles lit, songs played, aisle runner put in place. But the most important detail is the essential one: Is the bride ready? Until she is ready and in place, the wedding cannot begin no matter how many other details have been completed.

The Lord has been working upon me lately about the preparation of the bride of Christ for her wedding day. Scripture is clear in its presentation of the church as the bride of Christ. Revelation 19:7–8 is a beautiful picture of this couple and their wedding day: "'Let us rejoice and be glad and give him glory! For the wedding of the Lamb has come, and his bride has made herself ready. Fine linen, bright and clean, was given her to wear.' (Fine linen stands for the righteous acts of the saints.)"

Actually, the idea of the Lord being married to His people is not unique to the New Testament. The Old Testament writers often referred to Israel as a bride, pledged to be married to the Lord, the Bridegroom. Isaiah writes, "as a bridegroom rejoices over his bride, so will your God rejoice over you" (62:5).

Jeremiah also uses this imagery. "I remember the devotion of your youth, how as a bride you loved me and followed me through the desert, through a land not sown. Does a maiden forget her jewelry, a bride her wedding ornaments? Yet my people have forgotten me, days without number" (Jeremiah 2:2, 32).

How could God express in any better way His desire for intimacy with His people than to use the illustration of a man and woman who court and then are betrothed to one another, finally resulting in a wedding and the consummation of their union? Throughout Scripture, this is God's expressed desire and ultimate purpose for His people.

As I have been studying the Scriptures that relate to this powerful picture of the Lord and His people, I've become more and more aware of the need to prepare the bride for her wedding day. As we move closer to the day of the Lord's return, this becomes an increasingly urgent task. Referring again to Revelation 19:7, note two things about the preparation of the bride. First, she will be ready for the wedding. Second, she has prepared herself for the wedding: "For the wedding of the Lamb has come, and his bride has made herself ready."

Without being critical, does it seem to you today that the church, the bride of Christ, is ready for the wedding? If not, then it is time to begin this preparatory work. It is time to prepare the bride for her wedding day!

What does it mean for the bride to be prepared to meet the Bridegroom? It would probably take a book to answer that completely, but I believe we can make some movement toward understanding this by looking at just a couple of Scripture passages that teach eternal truths about the bride and the Bridegroom.

First, a key to preparation is understanding the issue of ownership or belonging. In the first part of John 3:29, we read, "The bride belongs to the bridegroom." Most cultures today are not comfortable with the idea of the marriage relationship being one of ownership of one person by another. But we do understand what it means to belong to someone. There is not just a legal connection, but a passionate emotional attachment.

The church, as the bride of Christ, belongs to Jesus. It is not only a legal issue accomplished at Calvary, but it is also a matter of the heart. It is a love relationship in which no other love or desire may enter to mar or damage the relationship. I remember singing the hymn "Now I Belong to Jesus" many times as I was growing up. It is time for the church to realize that we belong to Him and begin to nurture that love relationship.

Another truth about preparation of the bride of Christ is found in Peter's second epistle as he teaches about the second coming of Christ. He writes, "So then, dear friends, since you are looking forward to this, make every effort to be found spotless, blameless and at peace with him" (3:14). Peter gives us these very practical areas of preparation for the wedding of Christ and His people. This passage is one of the reasons I believe a great revival is coming for the church. A revived church is one that is consciously turning from sin in repentance and longing to be found spotless and blameless. A revived church has submitted to the lordship and authority of Christ and will be at peace with her Bridegroom.

The apostle John saw a vision of a prepared bride: "I saw the Holy City, the new Jerusalem, coming down out of heaven from God, prepared as a bride beautifully dressed for her husband" (Revelation 21:2). Is that a passion of your life yet? Are you committed to seeing the church prepared for the coming of her Bridegroom, the Lord Jesus?

As I was praying and studying over this topic, one particular day I was taught something hard by the Lord. In the midst of a prayer time, I pictured in my mind's eye a bride standing by the altar, waiting for the bridegroom. But as I continued in prayer, there came one of those sacred moments in which the Lord placed a thought in my mind and made the simple statement: "The bride is not at the altar yet."

It was a simple statement of fact, yet also a rebuke and an encouragement. The church—the bride—is not at the altar waiting for the Bridegroom. The bride is off doing a multitude of things, but very little of it concerns waiting at the altar for her Beloved. The rebuke was clear, but so was the encouragement.

It is time to bring the bride to the altar. It is time for the church to become a house of prayer. The kneeling church becomes the bride at the altar, prepared for the Bridegroom. "The Spirit and the bride say, 'Come!'" (Revelation 22:17).

PRAYER

Lord Jesus, please come soon for Your bride. Help us to become the pure and spotless bride in every way. Show me, Lord, the things in my life that hinder the body of Christ from being all that You have called us to be. Help me to grow in love for You and in greater desire for Your appearing.

QUESTIONS FOR REFLECTION AND DISCUSSION

1. Do you believe the church is prepared for the return of Jesus? If not, what needs to happen?

2. How can you pray in such a way that the church, the bride of Christ, becomes more prepared for her wedding day?

3. Do you think that the church is lacking in her love for the Bridegroom, Jesus? What do you believe can stir us up to love Jesus more deeply?

Chapter Eleven

PRAYING WITH URGENCY

I will always remember November 11, 1997. It was a holiday, so my family and I went to Indianapolis to relax and do some shopping. After a full day, we went to the airport to pick up some relatives and drive them back to Terre Haute. My mother's brother was waiting there for us. He had driven to the airport to give us the news that my mother had suffered a major stroke earlier that day. Suddenly, getting back home was an urgent matter. We drove quickly and went straight to the hospital.

Certain things in life can bring a sense of urgency. It may be something as mundane as hunger or thirst, or a crisis such as a medical emergency. When circumstances move together to create that urgency, suddenly everything changes. The normal things we do are laid aside and we focus all our attention on that which has created the tension or crisis in our lives. Urgency causes shifts in priorities and activities. Previously important activities fade into the background.

REMEMBERING TIME IS SHORT

I believe God is calling the church to a new sense of urgency. It is time to lay aside the normal routine. In one sense, this is the way the church has been called to live at all times. In another way, this sense of urgency is for God's people today.

The Bible teaches much about time and the Christian's wise use of it. One of the clearest teachings in Scripture regarding time is that it is limited for humans. We have only a relatively short time to live on this planet. Therefore, it is important that we make the most of every opportunity. Consider these passages:

- "We are aliens and strangers in your sight, as were all our forefathers. Our days on earth are like a shadow, without hope" (1 Chronicles 29:15).
- "You have made my days a mere handbreadth; the span of my years is as nothing before you. Each man's life is but a breath" (Psalm 39:5).
- "Whatever your hand finds to do, do it with all your might, for in the grave, where you are going, there is neither working nor planning nor knowledge nor wisdom" (Ecclesiastes 9:10).

Time is considered a gift from God and is intended to be used in a way that brings glory to Him. Ponder these texts:

- "Teach us to number our days aright, that we may gain a heart of wisdom" (Psalm 90:12).
- "Be very careful, then, how you live—not as unwise but as wise, making the most of every opportunity, because the days are evil" (Ephesians 5:15–16).
- "Be wise in the way you act toward outsiders; make the most of every opportunity" (Colossians 4:5).

Sometimes this shortness of time is expressed in relationship to the coming of the Lord to bring all time to an end: "What I mean, brothers, is that the time is short. From now on those who have wives should live as if they had none; those who mourn, as if they did not; those who are happy, as if they were not; those who buy something, as if it were not theirs to keep; those who use the things of the world, as if not engrossed in them. For this world in its present form is passing away" (1 Corinthians 7:29–31).

Urgency in the Bible is sometimes connected to both the completion of a task and a passion that connects us to God. I believe the following passage speaks strongly to us today of that situation: "For Zion's sake I will not keep silent, for Jerusalem's sake I will not remain quiet, till her righteousness shines out like the dawn, her salvation like a blazing torch" (Isaiah 62:1). Isaiah had begun to sense God's heart for His people. Through drawing near in prayer, the prophet's heart was lining up with God's heart. Many times the Lord had revealed His unfailing love for Israel and His desire for His people to return to Him. Isaiah began to pray the Lord's agenda, and it was a prayer of passion and urgency.

It is easy to allow our attention to be diverted back to what we call "normal." Unfortunately, normal often means life without God and without a dependence upon Him in prayer. I believe it is vital for us to hold onto our first response—the response of prayer.

The church desperately needs both to issue and respond to a new call for extraordinary prayer. Extraordinary prayer goes beyond the normal expectations of the past. It is prayer that can bring God's power to bear on a whole new world facing us—a world of uncertainty, fears, and war.

The Bible records times of extraordinary prayer like this. One good example occurred in the book of Esther. The crisis there concerned the lives of every Jew held captive in Babylon. A decree had been issued that would result in genocide for the Jews. Queen Esther was going to risk her life by going to the king on behalf of her people; however, before she went, she called her people to fast and pray with her for three days. Extraordinary prayer brought about extraordinary deliverance.

The book of Ezra gives another good example of extraordinary prayer. Ezra was preparing to lead a group of the exiles from Babylon back to Jerusalem. The king had even offered troops for protection on the perilous journey. But Ezra had refused the troops, pointing out that God Himself would protect them. As the people gathered, Ezra began to realize how dangerous the trip would be and that they should not merely presume upon God's protection. So he called the people to humble themselves and pray and fast over the journey. God heard their prayers and gave them safe passage to their destination.

There are many examples of urgent prayer in more recent history. The great British preacher Charles H. Spurgeon was used by God to bring many into the kingdom, and in the process a large church was built in London. Spurgeon challenged his people to extraordinary prayer if they wanted to see God's hand at work in their church. He wrote, quoted from www.watchword.org:

> Dear Friends, we do not know what God may do for us if we do but pray for a blessing of the Holy Spirit. . . . Have we not tried to preach without trying to pray? Is it not likely that the church has been putting forth its preaching hand but not its praying hand? O Dear friends! Let us agonize in prayer, and it shall come to pass that this Music Hall shall witness the sighs and groans of

the penitent and the songs of the converted. It shall yet happen that this vast host shall not come and go as now it does, but little the better; but men shall go out of this hall praising God and saying—It was good to be there; it was none other than the house of God, and the very gate of heaven. This much to stir you up to prayer.

In the United States, the revivals known as the great awakenings came in response to Christians gathering for extraordinary prayer. Often called "concerts of prayer," God used these times of prayer to bring awakening to His people. Robert Bakke, in his wonderful book *The Power of Extraordinary Prayer,* explains it this way:

> [The concert of prayer] was born out of convictions that say with certainty that, regardless of how bright or dark the hour we live in, God is about to do something greater than He's ever done before. Furthermore, it said that God would not move forward with His ever-increasing and ever more marvelous plans until Christians agreed with Him and agreed with each other about what He was going to do. A great and lucid vision of Christ's earthly reign was before their eyes—with every nation, people, tribe and tongue united as one company before the throne of God, Christ the Son, and the sevenfold Spirit. It was a compelling vision that would not let Christians rest or let go of God until the rule of God held sway in every aspect of life. (p. 133)

Read again that last sentence from Bakke: "It was a compelling vision that would not let Christians rest or let go of God until the rule of God held sway in every aspect of life." Have you ever made a decision to pray like that? Not merely saying, "God bless us" or even "God protect us," but a life-changing commitment to pray until the "rule of God held sway in every aspect of life"? This should not be just a response made only by individual Christians. Has your church made a decision to pray extraordinarily for the working of God's power? The key to the concert of prayer was for Christians to gather together for times of extraordinary prayer—as was the practice of the early church.

MAKING GOD'S PASSION OUR OWN

It is time today for the people of God to begin to hear God's heart so that we may pray with passion about that which God is passionate about. As we draw near to Him in prayer and in His Word, we find there are two things today that ought to bring a strong sense of urgency to the church: (1) the revival of the church, and (2) the completion of the task of world evangelization.

God earnestly desires a bride for His Son who is pure and spotless, and without blemish. This certainly will require a massive change on the part of the church that could only happen through heaven-sent revival. This bride is to be comprised of people from every tongue, tribe, and nation. The revival of the church and resulting completion of the task of world evangelization come from the very passions of God and require us to take up this task with urgency.

The church can begin by praying for and with the urgency and passion of Isaiah. This time, we pray for the new Zion, the new Jerusalem, the people of God. Like the prophet of old, we too must say, "I cannot remain silent. I will not stop praying for her until her righteousness shines like the dawn, and her salvation blazes like a burning torch" (Isaiah 62:1, NLT). We must lay aside lesser things. The call is for today. It is a call for the people of God to pray urgently with the heart of God for our generation.

PRAYER

"Rise up, O Church of God!
Have done with lesser things;
Give heart and mind and soul and strength
To serve the King of Kings."
　　　　—William P. Merrill, "Rise Up, O Church of God"

QUESTIONS FOR REFLECTION AND DISCUSSION

1. Do you believe we are living in the last days? If so, how should that belief change our lifestyles?

2. Are you comfortable with your priorities regarding the use of time? If not, what changes do you need to make and what would it take for you to make them?

3. Where is prayer in your priorities? What changes can or should you make in your prayer life?

Chapter Twelve

THE TRIUMPHAL ENTRY . . . AGAIN!

J esus was aware of His Father's timing. Everything He did and every move He made was under the direction of His heavenly Father and according to His schedule. It is because of the Father's agenda that Jesus scrupulously avoided declaring Himself Messiah in an open way. If He had done so earlier, the Jewish authorities would have tried to kill Him before His task was accomplished.

When it became apparent that the Father's perfect timing had arrived for Messiah to be revealed, however, Jesus set His face toward Jerusalem with a determination that would not be denied. The triumphal entry of Jesus into Jerusalem was a planned event. The waiting donkey demonstrated the Lord's planning. He anticipated the crowd's reaction to His appearance. In a subtle but clear way, Jesus declared His Messiahship by riding on that animal.

The crowds of Jerusalem responded just as He anticipated. They honored Him as Messiah and broke into the long-awaited cry, "Hosanna. . . . Blessed is he who comes in the name of the Lord!" (Matthew 21:9). With palm leaves and branches and cloaks spread in His path, riding on a donkey, the Prince of Peace entered His city.

When Jesus saw Jerusalem spread out before Him, He began to weep. With His prophetic insight He saw what would happen to Jerusalem in just forty years. Utter destruction. An event of such devastation that it was said that not one stone would remain upon another. It was, however, an event that could have been prevented had the rulers of Jerusalem recognized their King as He rode through their gates.

Jesus the Messiah entered Jerusalem recognized by a few, but rejected by the leaders and most of the people. This should not have happened. The Old Testament prophets had accurately foretold the coming of Messiah in such detail that the Jews should have been at the gates of Jerusalem on that exact day waiting expectantly for His appearance.

What kept them from receiving their Messiah was their focus on their traditions, as well as the long time between the prophecies and its fulfillment. Centuries of waiting had dulled their expectations of God's Anointed One coming among them. Maintaining religious traditions became paramount. Even God's actual coming could not move them from peering at the shadow while the reality walked in their midst.

Israel's failure to recognize Jesus as her Messiah resulted in the eventual destruction of Jerusalem and the dispersal of the Jewish people among the nations. As the time of the Gentiles has begun to approach its end, the Father has drawn the Jewish people back into the land of their ancestors.

In these last days, the people of God again await the triumphal entry of Messiah. King Jesus will once again enter Jerusalem. This time He is coming not as the unrecognized Lamb of God, but as the triumphant returning King with the angel armies of God at His back. Not only will Jerusalem behold His coming but also literally will the eyes of everyone on planet Earth.

Most of the people living on earth will be taken by surprise at this next triumphal entry, just like those in Jerusalem two thousand years ago. Some, however, were ready and waving palm branches in anticipation of their Messiah's arrival. So it shall be again. We are called as the church of Jesus Christ to live in joyful anticipation of His coming.

There is much unnecessary confusion about the return of Jesus. Many do not even anticipate His return because we will not know the day or the hour (Matthew 25:13). The Bible, however, doesn't allow us to shrug off His coming as though it is something of which we can know nothing. Paul wrote to the Thessalonians and told them that "the day of the Lord will come like a thief in the night" (1 Thessalonians 5:2). Just a few verses later he reminded them, "But you, brothers, are not in darkness so that this day should surprise you like a thief" (1 Thessalonians 5:4).

The clear teaching of Scripture is that those who are asleep, living in the darkness, will be surprised by the Lord's return. But there is a generation of Christians who will choose to live not in the darkness but in the day (1 Thessalonians 5:5). The hour or the day will not be revealed to them, but the season of His return will become increasingly apparent.

These will be the Annas and Simeons of our day. They will seek the face of the Lord and cry out for His coming. Because His Word is precious to them, they will recognize with increased clarity, the signs of His appearing.

Perhaps, most importantly, the generation that is waiting for the Lord's final triumphant entry will clothe themselves in holiness and purity as they prepare for the coming of the great Bridegroom. Peter wrote to those who are anticipating Jesus' second coming: "Since everything will be destroyed in this way, what kind of people ought you to be? You ought to live holy and godly lives as you look forward to the day of God and speed its coming" (2 Peter 3:11–12a).

If our eagerness for the Lord's return does not result in a radical change in lifestyle, we have somehow drifted from our biblical moorings. Concern about dates and times becomes meaningless speculation unless accompanied by lives of holiness and godliness. Jesus the Bridegroom is coming back for a bride who has prepared and clothed herself in spotless garments of white, signifying lives of purity and holiness.

Are you ready for His return? Will you be among those who have been stirred up by the Spirit and the Word to line the highway with palm branches and cries of praise? Look up, for your redemption draws near, church of God!

PRAYER

Lord, how eager I am for Your soon return! Please help me to discern the signs of Your coming. I don't want to be taken unaware by Your appearing. Pour out a spirit of watchful prayer upon me that I may be used by You to prayerfully prepare the way for Your triumphal return to this planet.

QUESTIONS FOR REFLECTION AND DISCUSSION

1. Do you agree that Christians should be able to discern the season of the Lord's return? Why or why not?

2. Do you believe that we are in the season of the Lord's return?

How does that belief impact your life?

3. Do you believe that God might be calling you to be like Anna or Simeon, one who is daily watching and interceding for the Lord's return? How can you make sure that you are prepared and ready for Jesus' appearing?

Chapter 13

PRAYING THE WILL OF GOD

zekiel 22:30 is a passage of Scripture that illustrates this principle of how the Lord works. "I looked for a man among them who would build up the wall and stand before me in the gap on behalf of the land so I would not have to destroy it, but I found none." God uses the illustration of a walled city to demonstrate His commitment to prayer. The walls protect a city from enemy attack. But through neglect (sin), the walls can begin to crumble and a gap or opening in the wall can create a dangerous situation where the enemy can come in. God said of Israel in Ezekiel's day, that she had allowed such a situation to develop. It was going to result in the destruction of the land, unless someone stood before the Lord in the gap on behalf of the land. This is a clear picture of God's desire for us to engage in intercessory prayer.

What is absolutely heartbreaking is that God Himself was looking for an intercessor. He was looking for someone who would stand before Him in prayer on behalf of Israel so that He would not have to destroy her because of sin and rebellion. God's desire is made clear here. He did not want to destroy Israel. He was waiting for an intercessor so He wouldn't have to. God had chosen to reserve His power to save the nation of Israel for those who prayed. But no intercessor was to be found. Israel was defeated by the Babylonians and her people were in exile for 70 years.

Isaiah 59 reflects a similar situation. The chapter speaks of a nation that was in trouble. There was no justice, violence was in the streets and the righteous were being preyed upon by the wicked. Verses 15 and 16 show us the Lord's response to the evil that was going on. "The LORD looked and was displeased that there was no justice. He saw that there was no one, he was appalled that there was no one to intercede."

Once again, the Lord made His will very clear. He was displeased by what was happening in Israel and desired for matters to be made right. He was waiting for His people to pray, so that salvation and righteousness might be poured out upon the people. But again, there was no one to intercede. In this case, however, the Lord allowed Israel to suffer in sin for hundreds of years until His people were redeemed by the coming of the Messiah. God always looks first for an intercessor. It is His plan to accomplish His will on this planet through the prayers of the saints.

It is for this reason that Jesus taught us to pray, "Your will be done on earth as it is in heaven." God has given us the awesome privilege of partnering with Him in bringing about the advance of His kingdom on earth. As we ask ourselves, "why pray?" we can move from a lethargic attitude about prayer to a place of tremendous excitement as we join with God in what He is doing on this planet.

It is exactly that understanding that our prayers are all about what God is doing, that also makes it sometimes very difficult to know how to pray in contemporary situations. What if what God is doing, or allowing Satan to do, in preparation for the return of Jesus, will in fact create dangerous and even cataclysmic events in our day?

Will we have the courage to still pray, "Your will be done"?

My friend and colleague Jon Graf, has written a thought-provoking essay on this topic that just might shake your world. Please prayerfully consider how you would pray in the circumstances he presents.

In the April 6, 2006 TIME magazine, essayist Charles Krauthammer wrote about the dangers of Iran gaining nuclear power. Basing his comments on President Ahmadinejad's speeches, he said for the first time we have a world leader, with nuclear power, who views himself as someone who can light the fuse for the chaotic end of the world. "[Ahmadinejad] is a fervent believer in the imminent reappearance of the 12th Imam, Shi'ism's version of the Messiah," who, said Krauthammer, will come following this time of chaos. And Ahmadinejad believes this period is only two to three years away.

For those of us who long to see Jesus Christ's second coming, Ahmadinejad's words have to make us think. Christian minds are already racing on how this fits in with end-time scenarios. And as this situation with Iran continues to play out, our minds will continually go to this issue. But I have a question: How should we respond in prayer?

No one in their right mind wants to see a nuclear holocaust destroy entire cities. Certainly most would try to pray against this madman and what his actions might cause catastrophically. It is a natural reaction to pray for our lives to be safe and normal. But safe and normal seldom do much for the kingdom! What if his evil actions will be used by God to eventually usher in the second coming? If we pray against it, aren't we praying against God's will?

As I read the TIME essay, I pondered this question. We want our prayers to reflect God's heart and purposes. And remember, God often uses Satan's evil activities for His good. So this is what I came up with.

1. Pray that as people see the world becoming more and more chaotic, their hearts would be open to the love of Jesus Christ. Pray that every evil action of Satan would bring multitudes into the kingdom of light.

2. Pray that believers would start living as true believers. That we would truly become salt and light to a dark world. As David Bryant put it, pray for a "re-conversion of God's people back to God's Son for all that He is." Pray that in these latter days both we and our children would stop putting ease of life in front of spreading the gospel.

3. Pray that our people and churches worldwide would live as if the second coming of Christ were just around the corner! That our lives, our finances, our sacrifices would reflect this renewed passion.

4. Above all pray for the glory of Jesus Christ to be revealed to the nations!

We long to see the King of kings return. But we have to remember that Jesus' return is tied into the completion of the Great Commission. He will only return when the last people group hears the gospel, when the last person who will believe, does believe. Our prayers regarding current events should always reflect that! (Prayer Leader OnLine, August 2006)

The issue of praying the Lord's will is absolutely critical for us as we approach the end of days. If we continue to incorrectly see prayer as a way to get what we want from God, we will never be used by God to accomplish His purposes through prayer. We must passionately desire the Lord's Presence and the fulfillment of His purposes, regardless of the cost. That will require disciplined, focused praying that pays careful attention to the Word of God.

PRAYER

Father, please teach me to pray Your will. Help me to have greater clarity and understanding as I pray over my world and Your activity in the world. Give me the courage to pray about things that might not be easy or pleasant. I want to pray that Your will would be done on earth as it is in heaven.

QUESTIONS FOR REFLECTION AND DISCUSSION

1. Do you believe that God is waiting for us to pray before He acts? How have you experienced that in your life?

2. Is there a particular way that you have learned to focus on God's will as you pray? What do you do?

3. As you look at current world events, is there something taking place that you believe is an indication of God at work? What is it? How has it prompted you to pray?

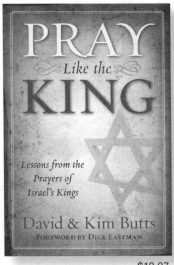

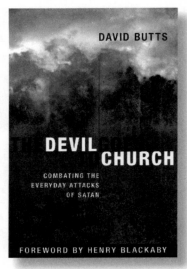